HARCOURT Social Studies

WITHDRAWN

World Regions

Activity Book

HARCOURT
SCHOOL PUBLISHERS
www.harcourtschool.com

ISBN-13: 978-0-15-356687-5
ISBN-10: 0-15-356687-6

4 5 6 7 8 9 10 018 09

The activities in this book reinforce social studies concepts and skills in *Harcourt Horizons: World Regions*. There is one activity for every lesson and skill in the Pupil Edition. Copies of the activity pages appear with answers in the Teacher's Edition. In addition to activities, this book also contains reproductions of the graphic organizers that appear in the chapter reviews in the Pupil Edition. Multiple-choice test preparation pages for student practice are also provided. A blank multiple-choice answer sheet can be found after these table of contents pages.

Contents

Introduction

viii   **Multiple-Choice Answer Sheet**
1   Skills: Read a Map
3   Why Geography Matters
4   Why History Matters
5   Skills: Compare Primary and Secondary Sources
6   Why Culture and Society, Civics and Government, and Economics Matter

Chapter 1

7   Lesson 1: Earth's Landforms
8   Lesson 2: Earth's Bodies of Water
9   Skills: Use Latitude and Longitude
11   Lesson 3: Earth's Climate and Vegetation
12   Lesson 4: Natural Resources
13   Skills: Solve a Problem
14   **Chapter Review**
15   **Test Preparation**

Chapter 2

16   Lesson 1: Population and Settlement
17   Skills: Read a Population Map
19   Lesson 2: Cultures and Societies
20   Skills: Read Parallel Time Lines
22   Lesson 3: Governments and Economies
23   Lesson 4: Looking at Regions
24   Skills: Identify National Symbols
25   **Chapter Review**
26   **Test Preparation**

·UNIT·

2

Chapter 3

27   Lesson 1: From Sea to Shining Sea
28   Skills: Read a Relief and Elevation Map
30   Lesson 2: A New Republic
31   Lesson 3: One People, Many Cultures
32   Skills: Determine Point of View
33   Lesson 4: Let Freedom Ring
34   Skills: Make Economic Choices
35   **Chapter Review**
36   **Test Preparation**

Chapter 4

37   Lesson 1: Land and the People
39   Lesson 2: Through the Centuries
40   Lesson 3: Canada's Government
41   Skills: Follow a Flow Chart
43   **Chapter Review**
44   **Test Preparation**

·UNIT·

3

Chapter 5

45   Lesson 1: A Rugged Land
47   Lesson 2: Creating a Mexican Culture
48   Lesson 3: Yesterday and Today
49   Skills: Identify Cause and Effect
51   **Chapter Review**
52   **Test Preparation**

Chapter 6

53   Lesson 1: Mountains, Volcanoes, Islands, and Hurricanes
55   Lesson 2: Influences of the Past
57   Lesson 3: Contrasts in Governing
58   Skills: Make a Thoughtful Decision
59   **Chapter Review**
60   **Test Preparation**

Chapter 7

61   Lesson 1: A Vast Land
63   Skills: Read a Map of Cultural Regions
65   Lesson 2: Cultures and Lifeways
66   Skills: Read a Double-Bar Graph
68   Lesson 3: Building a Future
69   **Chapter Review**
70   **Test Preparation**

·UNIT· 4

Chapter 8
71 Lesson 1: Islands, Peninsulas, and Mountains
73 Skills: Land Use and Products
75 Lesson 2: Western Europe Through the Ages
76 Lesson 3: Culture Unites and Culture Divides
77 Lesson 4: Unity in Europe
78 Skills: Read an Editorial Cartoon
79 **Chapter Review**
80 **Test Preparation**

Chapter 9
81 Lesson 1: Varied Lands and Varied Resources
83 Lesson 2: Centuries of Change
84 Skills: Identify Changing Borders
86 Lesson 3: Times of Freedom
87 Lesson 4: Varied Cultures
88 Skills: Resolve Conflicts
89 **Chapter Review**
90 **Test Preparation**

Chapter 10
91 Lesson 1: Landforms and Climates
92 Skills: Read a Climograph
94 Lesson 2: The Soviet Union Rises and Falls
95 Skills: Read a Time Zone Map
97 Lesson 3: Times of Change
98 **Chapter Review**
99 **Test Preparation**

·UNIT· 5

Chapter 11
100 Lesson 1: Land of Contrasts
101 Lesson 2: Southwest Asia Long Ago
102 Skills: Compare Historical Maps
104 Lesson 3: Influences on Cultures
105 Lesson 4: New Governments and Strong Economies
106 Skills: Identify Frames of Reference
107 **Chapter Review**
108 **Test Preparation**

Chapter 12
109 Lesson 1: A Region of Deserts
110 Skills: Follow Routes on a Map
112 Lesson 2: Ancient Days to Independence
113 Skills: Read a Telescoping Time Line

115 Lesson 3: A Blend of Cultures
116 Lesson 4: Present-Day Concerns
117 Chapter Review
118 Test Preparation

·UNIT· 6

Chapter 13
119 Lesson 1: Desert, Savanna, and Rain Forest
121 Skills: Compare Map Projections
123 Lesson 2: A Time of Empires
124 Skills: Identify Fact and Opinion
125 Lesson 3: Many Cultures
126 Lesson 4: Developing Nations
127 Chapter Review
128 Test Preparation

Chapter 14
129 Lesson 1: Plains and Plateaus
131 Lesson 2: Ancient Cultures
132 Lesson 3: From Colonies to Countries
133 Lesson 4: Facing the Future
134 Skills: Compare Tables
136 Chapter Review
137 Test Preparation

·UNIT· 7

Chapter 15
138 Lesson 1: Great Rivers, Mighty Monsoons
139 Lesson 2: Through the Ages
140 Lesson 3: People and Culture
141 Skills: Predict a Likely Outcome
142 Lesson 4: South Asia Today
143 Skills: Read a Population Pyramid
145 Chapter Review
146 Test Preparation

Chapter 16
147 Lesson 1: Mountains, Deserts, Rivers, and Seas
148 Lesson 2: Long-Lasting Civilizations
149 Skills: Read a Cartogram
151 Lesson 3: A Life of Traditions and Religions
152 Lesson 4: A Region of Contrasts
153 Chapter Review
154 Test Preparation

Chapter 17

155 Lesson 1: Peninsulas, Islands, and Seas

156 Skills: Compare Maps of Different Scale

158 Lesson 2: In the Shadow of Others

159 Lesson 3: Varying Economies, Varying Governments

160 Skills: Compare Circle Graphs

162 **Chapter Review**

163 **Test Preparation**

·UNIT·

8

Chapter 18

164 Lesson 1: The Lands Down Under

165 Lesson 2: Outposts in the Pacific

166 Skills: Act as a Responsible Citizen

167 Lesson 3: Australia and New Zealand Today

168 Skills: Compare Line Graphs

170 Chapter Review

171 Test Preparation

Chapter 19

172 Lesson 1: Island Migrations

174 Lesson 2: Island Nations

175 Skills: Compare Different Kinds of Maps

177 Lesson 3: Antarctica: A Continent Without a Population

179 Chapter Review

180 Test Preparation

Multiple-Choice
Answer Sheet

**Number your answers to match the questions
on the test preparation page.**

____ Ⓐ Ⓑ Ⓒ Ⓓ
____ Ⓕ Ⓖ Ⓗ Ⓙ
____ Ⓐ Ⓑ Ⓒ Ⓓ
____ Ⓕ Ⓖ Ⓗ Ⓙ
____ Ⓐ Ⓑ Ⓒ Ⓓ

____ Ⓐ Ⓑ Ⓒ Ⓓ
____ Ⓕ Ⓖ Ⓗ Ⓙ
____ Ⓐ Ⓑ Ⓒ Ⓓ
____ Ⓕ Ⓖ Ⓗ Ⓙ
____ Ⓐ Ⓑ Ⓒ Ⓓ

____ Ⓐ Ⓑ Ⓒ Ⓓ
____ Ⓕ Ⓖ Ⓗ Ⓙ
____ Ⓐ Ⓑ Ⓒ Ⓓ
____ Ⓕ Ⓖ Ⓗ Ⓙ
____ Ⓐ Ⓑ Ⓒ Ⓓ

____ Ⓐ Ⓑ Ⓒ Ⓓ
____ Ⓕ Ⓖ Ⓗ Ⓙ
____ Ⓐ Ⓑ Ⓒ Ⓓ
____ Ⓕ Ⓖ Ⓗ Ⓙ
____ Ⓐ Ⓑ Ⓒ Ⓓ

____ Ⓐ Ⓑ Ⓒ Ⓓ
____ Ⓕ Ⓖ Ⓗ Ⓙ
____ Ⓐ Ⓑ Ⓒ Ⓓ
____ Ⓕ Ⓖ Ⓗ Ⓙ
____ Ⓐ Ⓑ Ⓒ Ⓓ

____ Ⓐ Ⓑ Ⓒ Ⓓ
____ Ⓕ Ⓖ Ⓗ Ⓙ
____ Ⓐ Ⓑ Ⓒ Ⓓ
____ Ⓕ Ⓖ Ⓗ Ⓙ
____ Ⓐ Ⓑ Ⓒ Ⓓ

____ Ⓐ Ⓑ Ⓒ Ⓓ
____ Ⓕ Ⓖ Ⓗ Ⓙ
____ Ⓐ Ⓑ Ⓒ Ⓓ
____ Ⓕ Ⓖ Ⓗ Ⓙ
____ Ⓐ Ⓑ Ⓒ Ⓓ

____ Ⓐ Ⓑ Ⓒ Ⓓ
____ Ⓕ Ⓖ Ⓗ Ⓙ
____ Ⓐ Ⓑ Ⓒ Ⓓ
____ Ⓕ Ⓖ Ⓗ Ⓙ
____ Ⓐ Ⓑ Ⓒ Ⓓ

____ Ⓐ Ⓑ Ⓒ Ⓓ
____ Ⓕ Ⓖ Ⓗ Ⓙ
____ Ⓐ Ⓑ Ⓒ Ⓓ
____ Ⓕ Ⓖ Ⓗ Ⓙ
____ Ⓐ Ⓑ Ⓒ Ⓓ

____ Ⓐ Ⓑ Ⓒ Ⓓ
____ Ⓕ Ⓖ Ⓗ Ⓙ
____ Ⓐ Ⓑ Ⓒ Ⓓ
____ Ⓕ Ⓖ Ⓗ Ⓙ
____ Ⓐ Ⓑ Ⓒ Ⓓ

____ Ⓐ Ⓑ Ⓒ Ⓓ
____ Ⓕ Ⓖ Ⓗ Ⓙ
____ Ⓐ Ⓑ Ⓒ Ⓓ
____ Ⓕ Ⓖ Ⓗ Ⓙ
____ Ⓐ Ⓑ Ⓒ Ⓓ

____ Ⓐ Ⓑ Ⓒ Ⓓ
____ Ⓕ Ⓖ Ⓗ Ⓙ
____ Ⓐ Ⓑ Ⓒ Ⓓ
____ Ⓕ Ⓖ Ⓗ Ⓙ
____ Ⓐ Ⓑ Ⓒ Ⓓ

____ Ⓐ Ⓑ Ⓒ Ⓓ
____ Ⓕ Ⓖ Ⓗ Ⓙ
____ Ⓐ Ⓑ Ⓒ Ⓓ
____ Ⓕ Ⓖ Ⓗ Ⓙ
____ Ⓐ Ⓑ Ⓒ Ⓓ

____ Ⓐ Ⓑ Ⓒ Ⓓ
____ Ⓕ Ⓖ Ⓗ Ⓙ
____ Ⓐ Ⓑ Ⓒ Ⓓ
____ Ⓕ Ⓖ Ⓗ Ⓙ
____ Ⓐ Ⓑ Ⓒ Ⓓ

____ Ⓐ Ⓑ Ⓒ Ⓓ
____ Ⓕ Ⓖ Ⓗ Ⓙ
____ Ⓐ Ⓑ Ⓒ Ⓓ
____ Ⓕ Ⓖ Ⓗ Ⓙ
____ Ⓐ Ⓑ Ⓒ Ⓓ

____ Ⓐ Ⓑ Ⓒ Ⓓ
____ Ⓕ Ⓖ Ⓗ Ⓙ
____ Ⓐ Ⓑ Ⓒ Ⓓ
____ Ⓕ Ⓖ Ⓗ Ⓙ
____ Ⓐ Ⓑ Ⓒ Ⓓ

____ Ⓐ Ⓑ Ⓒ Ⓓ
____ Ⓕ Ⓖ Ⓗ Ⓙ
____ Ⓐ Ⓑ Ⓒ Ⓓ
____ Ⓕ Ⓖ Ⓗ Ⓙ
____ Ⓐ Ⓑ Ⓒ Ⓓ

____ Ⓐ Ⓑ Ⓒ Ⓓ
____ Ⓕ Ⓖ Ⓗ Ⓙ
____ Ⓐ Ⓑ Ⓒ Ⓓ
____ Ⓕ Ⓖ Ⓗ Ⓙ
____ Ⓐ Ⓑ Ⓒ Ⓓ

Name _____   Date _____

MAP AND GLOBE SKILLS
Read a Map

Directions Maps are drawings that show places on Earth. A map can help you find the locations of countries, cities, landforms, and bodies of water. Maps have many special features that help you read the information they contain. Study the list of map features below. Some of the features have been correctly identified on the map. Fill in the missing names of features in the spaces below.

compass rose	inset map	map key	map title
grid	locator	map scale	

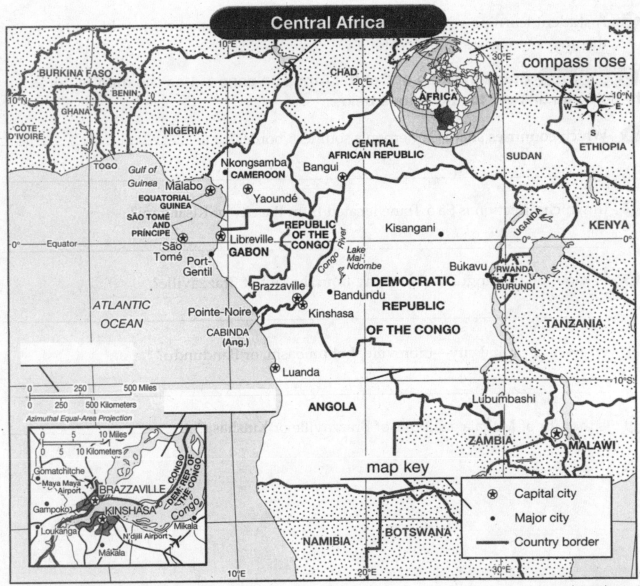

(continued)

© Harcourt

Name _____ Date _____

Directions Study the map of Central Africa on page 1. Then read each of the situations below. Underline the name of the correct map feature that helps to solve the problem.

1 A travel agent searching for a map of Central Africa would read the (map keys / map titles) to find the correct one.

2 A student would use a (compass rose / map key) to learn the direction of Equatorial Guinea from Luanda, Angola.

3 A cartographer would use a (map key / map scale) to figure out the distance between Kinshasa and Libreville.

4 A tourist who wants to find the location of the Kinshasa airport would use the (inset map / locator).

5 A student learning where Central Africa is located in the world would study the map's (compass rose / locator).

Directions Study the map of Central Africa on page 1. Use the map features to help you answer the questions below.

6 Which countries share Cameroon's southern border? _____
_____

7 In which direction is São Tomé located from the city of Kisangani?
_____

8 Is Yaoundé or Bangui farther away from the city of Brazzaville?
_____

9 Which is a capital city—Libreville, Lubumbashi, or Bandundu?
_____

10 Is the city of Makala a suburb of Brazzaville or Kinshasa? _____

Use after reading Skill Lesson, pages A2–A3.

© Harcourt

Name _____ Date _____

Why Geography Matters

Directions Geographers study Earth in different ways. Some geographers use five topics called the five themes of geography. Others use six topics called the six essential elements of geography. Review the pictures below. Then choose the theme or essential element that a geographer would think about if he or she was studying the information in the picture. Some questions may have more than one correct answer. Write the letters of the best answers on the lines next to the pictures.

1 _____

    A. Location
    B. Places and Regions
    C. Movement

2 _____

    A. Environment and Society
    B. The World in Spatial Terms
    C. Human-Environment Interactions

3 _____

    A. Places and Regions
    B. The World in Spatial Terms
    C. Location

4 _____

    A. Place
    B. Physical Systems
    C. Location

5 _____

    A. Physical Systems
    B. The Uses of Geography
    C. Places and Regions

Why History Matters

Directions Historians look for clues about the past when they study objects that people have left behind. Objects teach us about people's clothes, food, trade, and other parts of their daily lives. Imagine you are a historian who has just found an old Viking settlement. Your team has uncovered many objects. Study the objects and use them to answer the questions that follow.

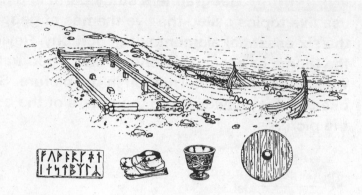

1 What do the ice skates teach us about the daily lives of the Viking people?

_____

_____

_____

_____

2 What do the shield and longship teach us about the Vikings?

_____

_____

_____

3 Why is the silver cup from Britain an important find? _____

_____

_____

4 What does the alphabet teach us about the Viking culture?

_____

_____

_____

Name _____   Date _____

READING SKILLS

Compare Primary and Secondary Sources

Directions Primary sources are firsthand accounts of historical events. Secondary sources are descriptions of events written later. Below are two accounts of the Japanese surrender that ended World War II. Read each source and compare them by answering the questions that follow.

From a radio message dated August 14, 1945, by Emperor Hirohito

After pondering deeply the general trends of the world and the actual conditions obtaining in Our Empire today, We have decided to effect a settlement of the present situation by resorting to an extraordinary measure. The war situation has developed not necessarily to Japan's advantage. Moreover, the enemy has begun to employ a new and most cruel bomb. Should We continue to fight, it would not only result in an ultimate collapse and obliteration of the Japanese nation, but also it would lead to the total extinction of human civilization. This is the reason why We have ordered the acceptance of the provisions of the Joint Declaration of the Powers.

A Country Study from the Library of Congress

After initial naval and battlefield successes and a tremendous over extension of its resources in the war . . . Japan was unable to sustain "Greater East Asia" [the Japanese Empire]. After the detonation of atomic bombs over Hiroshima and Nagasaki on August 6 and 8, 1945, the emperor asked that the Japanese people bring peace to Japan . . . by surrendering to the Allied powers. The documents of surrender were signed on board the U.S.S. Missouri in Tokyo Bay on September 2, 1945. The terms of surrender included the occupation of Japan by Allied military forces . . . and surrender of Japan's colonial holdings.

❶ Which source is the primary source? Explain how you know.

_____

_____

❷ Which of the sources gives more detail about the actual surrender of Japan?

_____

❸ Does the primary or secondary source have examples of bias within it? Explain

your answer. _____

_____

Why Culture and Society Matters/
Why Civics and Government Matters/
Why Economics Matters

Directions The statements below describe countries or regions you will learn about in your textbook. Decide if each of the statements refers to the culture, society, civic rights and responsibilities, government, or economy of the country or region. Write the vocabulary term that best describes the statement. Use your textbook to help you review the vocabulary before you begin.

Vocabulary
Civic rights and responsibilities
Culture
Economy
Government
Society

1 Today many South American countries have a middle class made up mostly of business workers and professional people. Most South Americans, however, belong to the lower classes.

_____

2 Brunei is a kind of monarchy called a sultanate. A leader called a sultan rules it. The sultan has a cabinet. _____

3 For many years, Mexicans worked in primary industries—farming and mining. In the 1940s, many Mexicans started working in manufacturing. Mexicans now manufacture many of the finished products they buy and use. _____

4 Australians speak English, but in their own special ways. They also adopted Aborigine words such as *jumbuck*, which means "sheep." _____

5 Australians and New Zealanders are aware of the importance of conserving their environments and wildlife. Environmentalists have influenced governments to protect the land and wildlife. _____

6 In China people are not allowed to say anything bad about the government. Newspapers and television stations are censored. This means they cannot print or broadcast anything the government does not allow. _____

7 In African villages, elders met to discuss problems and agree on solutions. Even in many cultures where a king led the people, a council of advisers made the most important decisions. _____

Use after reading Introduction Lesson, pages 8–10.

© Harcourt

Earth's Landforms

Directions Earth's surface changes in many ways. Weathering, erosion, and deposition affect Earth's shape. Human activities such as building structures and farming also change Earth. Review each of the definitions and study the landscape below. Then circle and label all the examples of weathering, erosion, deposition, and human activities that you can find in the landscape.

Weathering: The process of breaking up rocks into smaller pieces, or sediment, by water, glaciers, and wind

Erosion: The process of moving sediment

Deposition: The process of dropping sediment in a new location

Human Activities: Changes people make

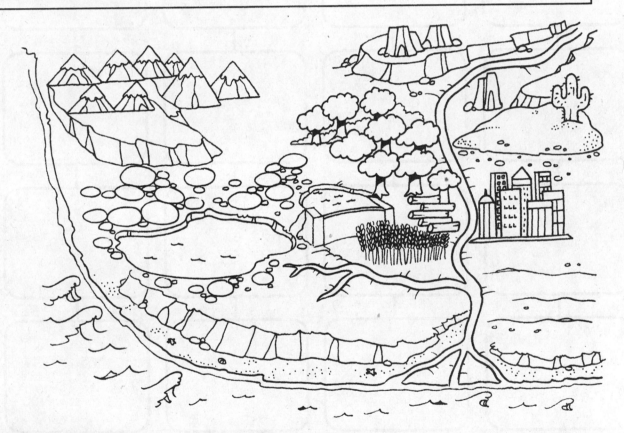

Directions Read the question. Write your answer on the lines provided.

How have human activities changed this landscape?

_____

_____

_____

Earth's Bodies of Water

Directions Earth has many different kinds of bodies of water. Read their names in the graphic organizer below. Then fill in the columns with statements that describe how bodies of water are formed and details that make each kind different from the others.

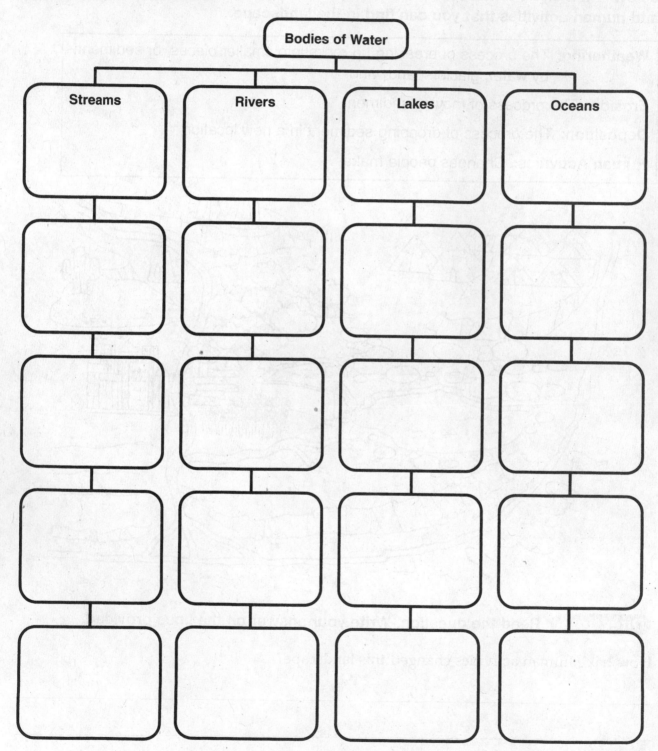

© Harcourt

MAP AND GLOBE SKILLS
Use Latitude and Longitude

Directions Study the map. Look closely at the lines of latitude and the lines of longitude. Then use the map to help you answer the questions that follow.

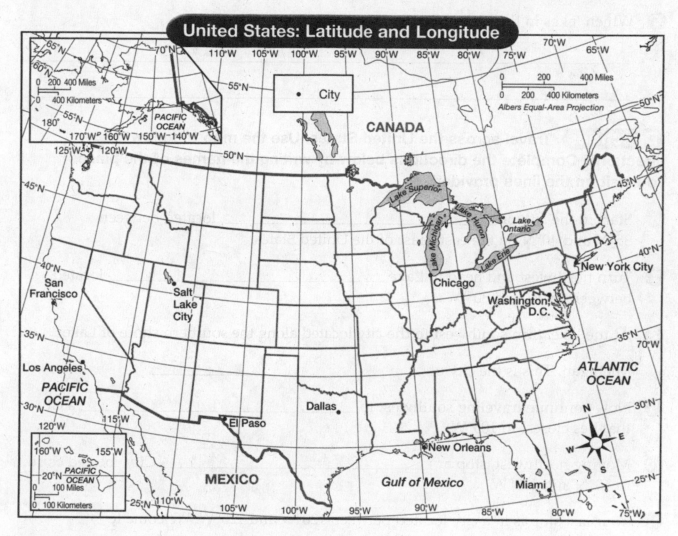

United States: Latitude and Longitude

1 Which city is located between 115°W and 120°W?

_____

2 Which city is located where 30°N and 90°W cross?

_____

(continued)

© Harcourt

3 Which city on the map is the closest to 40°N and 75°W?

_____

4 Which bodies of water does 25°N cross?

_____

5 Which lakes in the United States does 45°N pass through?

_____

_____

Directions Travel across the United States! Use the map to follow the directions. Complete the directions below by writing the names of the places you visit on the lines provided.

6 Start in the city of _____, located between 35°N and 40°N on the east coast of the United States.

7 Turn northwest and head to Lake _____, located between 75°W and 80°W.

8 At the lake, turn southwest to the city located along the southern shore of Lake

Michigan. This is the city of _____.

9 Now continue traveling southwest to _____, a city that lies closest to 105°W.

10 Moving northwest, stop at _____ City, located close to 40°N and 112°W.

11 Your last stop is in a city located between 120°W and 125°W. Welcome to

_____.

© Harcourt

Use after reading Chapter 1, Skill Lesson, pages 32–33.

Name _____ Date _____

Earth's Climates and Vegetation

Directions Read the following paragraph and study the diagram to help you answer the questions below.

    Climate is the kind of weather a place has over long periods of time. Altitude has a major effect on mountain climates. Every 1,000 feet (305m) the land rises, the air turns colder by 3 degrees Fahrenheit (1.7 degrees Celsius). Altitude also affects the climate of a place through the weather. As air rises over one side of the mountain, it turns colder and loses moisture in the form of rain and snow. As the now dry air passes over to the other side of the mountain, it drops closer to the ground and begins warming. As the air warms, it absorbs moisture from the land around it. This side of the mountain is called the rain shadow. The area affected by the rain shadow has a much drier climate.

1 How are the climate and land on the left side of the mountain different from the

climate and land on the right side? _____

_____

_____

2 How might the rain shadow affect human activities? _____

_____

_____

Name _____ Date _____

Natural Resources

Directions Underline the word or group of words in parentheses that best completes each sentence.

1 Graphite is a (mineral resource / biological resource) that is used to make pencils.

2 Fossil fuels are (renewable/nonrenewable) resources because they cannot be replaced within a reasonable time.

3 Using less water is one example of how people can (recycle/conserve) resources.

4 Some mineral resources called (chemicals/fossil fuels) are used to provide energy.

5 (Trees /Petroleum and gas) are resources that help clean the air and are a source of wood for homes and furniture.

Directions Match the energy descriptions on the left with the energy sources on the right.

Energy

6 _____ Electricity created by air flowing over a special engine called a turbine.

7 _____ This is energy created by the sun heating water and changing it into steam.

8 _____ The fuel produced from this is used to power automobiles around the world.

9 _____ Electricity made by water flowing over a turbine engine.

10 _____ This mineral resource is burned to create heat energy that heats homes.

11 _____ In many countries people burn this biological resource to heat their homes and cook their food.

Energy Sources

A. petroleum

B. tidal energy

C. wind power

D. solar power

E. coal

F. wood

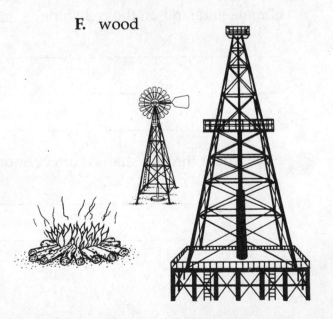

© Harcourt

Use after reading Chapter 1, Lesson 4, pages 40–45.

Name _____ Date _____

CITIZENSHIP SKILLS
Solve a Problem

Directions Read about the problem of water pollution and the five steps to solve it. Put the statements in order by writing the letter of each one next to the correct step in the problem-solving process.

Fresh water is an important natural resource that is automatically renewed by the water cycle. Water pollution prevents the water cycle from resupplying Earth with fresh water. Much of the water pollution comes from our own homes. Motor oil from leaking automobiles is swept into the sewer systems and pollutes the water of streams, rivers, and lakes. Water pollution damages marine life and the health of people and animals who drink it.

Solving the Water Pollution Problem

A. It would also be better for the environment to fix the motor oil leak. Parking the automobile away from the sewers will not stop it from polluting the water.

B. How do we prevent motor oil from our automobile from being washed down our driveways and causing water pollution?

C. We cleaned the oil from the driveway, we fixed the automobile so that it no longer leaks motor oil. The driveway is clean, and no motor oil is leaking into the sewer system.

D. Bring the car to a mechanic to fix the oil leak.

E. We can fix the automobiles to stop them from leaking motor oil, or we can park our automobiles away from the sewer system.

Problem-Solving Process

❶ _____ Identify the problem.

❷ _____ Think of possible solutions.

❸ _____ Look at the facts of the situation and compare how each solution would work.

❹ _____ Plan a way to carry out the solution.

❺ _____ Evaluate the solution and think about how well it solves the problem.

© Harcourt

Name _____ Date _____

The World's Geography

Directions Complete this graphic organizer to show that you understand how to identify the main idea and the supporting details for each lesson of Chapter 1.

$$\boxed{\text{MAIN IDEA}} \rightarrow \boxed{\text{DETAILS}}$$

LESSON 1 MAIN IDEA:

Earth's landforms have been shaped and reshaped over time.

Detail: _____

_____

_____

LESSON 3 MAIN IDEA:

Earth, the sun, the oceans, and the wind interact to produce Earth's varied climates.

Detail: _____

_____

_____

_____

The World's Geography

LESSON 2 MAIN IDEA:

Earth's bodies of water support life on the planet.

Detail: _____

_____

_____

_____

LESSON 4 MAIN IDEA:

Earth's natural resources are important to people.

Detail: _____

_____

_____

_____

© Harcourt

Use after reading Chapter 1, pages 18–49.

Name _____ Date _____

1 Test Preparation

Directions Read each question and choose the best answer. Then fill in the circle for the answer you have chosen. Be sure to fill in the circle completely.

1 What impact does a rain shadow have on the land below it?
- Ⓐ It causes Earth's tectonic plates to slide.
- Ⓑ It causes the air to rise over the land.
- Ⓒ It causes rain and snow to fall on the land.
- Ⓓ It causes the dry air to absorb moisture from the land.

2 The largest amount of fresh water can be found in—
- Ⓕ frozen glaciers and ice caps.
- Ⓖ water vapor in the air.
- Ⓗ dampness in the soil.
- Ⓙ lakes and rivers.

3 If it is summer in the Northern Hemisphere, then which statement is true?
- Ⓐ The Northern Hemisphere is tilted toward the sun.
- Ⓑ The Northern Hemisphere is entirely above the Tropic of Cancer.
- Ⓒ It is summer in the Southern Hemisphere, too.
- Ⓓ The sun's rays are vertical at 23.5 degrees south latitude.

4 A nonrenewable resource is—
- Ⓕ wind power.
- Ⓖ forests.
- Ⓗ water.
- Ⓙ oil and natural gas.

5 What effect do arid climates have on vegetation?
- Ⓐ Vegetation does not grow in arid climates.
- Ⓑ Vegetation grows in dense clusters.
- Ⓒ Vegetation grows far apart with long roots.
- Ⓓ Vegetation grows without roots.

© Harcourt

Population and Settlement

Directions Read the paragraph and study the chart below, which shows four circle graphs. Then use the chart to answer the questions.

The movement of people on Earth is called migration. Some people migrate, or leave, their homeland for economic opportunities and better lives. These people are known by international law as **immigrants.** Others are forced from their home by war and unfair treatment. These people are known as **refugees.** According to the United Nations, there have been about 22.3 million refugees in recent years. In many countries they make up a large part of the population. The circle graphs below show the total population of four countries and the percent of people who have been pushed from these places during 1999–2000.

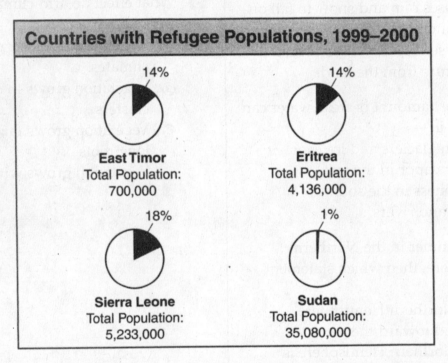

Countries with Refugee Populations, 1999–2000

14%
East Timor
Total Population:
700,000

14%
Eritrea
Total Population:
4,136,000

18%
Sierra Leone
Total Population:
5,233,000

1%
Sudan
Total Population:
35,080,000

❶ Which country had the largest percent of refugees? Which country had the smallest? _____

❷ Both Eritrea and East Timor lost 14 percent of their population. Which country had the greater number of citizens outside its borders? _____

❸ Look closely at the total population and the percent of refugees for these countries. Which country had the highest number of refugees? _____

_____

Name _____ Date _____

MAP AND GLOBE SKILLS
Read a Population Map

Directions Study the map below. Pay close attention to the population density patterns of Asia. Use the map and an atlas to help you complete the map.

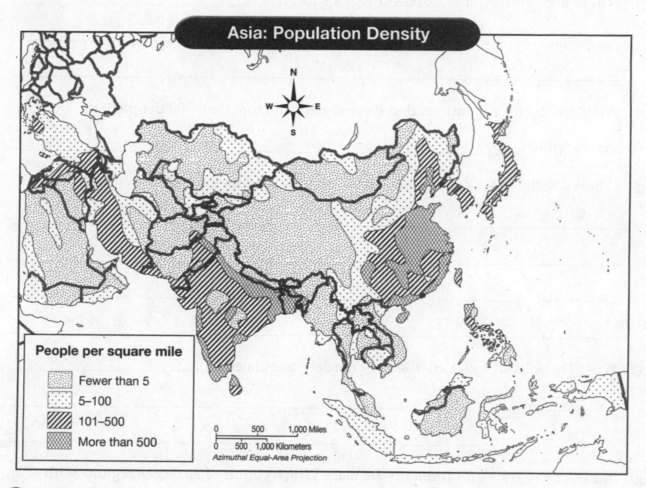

Asia: Population Density

People per square mile

Fewer than 5
5–100
101–500
More than 500

0   500   1,000 Miles
0   500 1,000 Kilometers
Azimuthal Equal-Area Projection

1. On the map, label the East Asian country that has fewer than 5 people per square mile in its western regions and more than 500 people per square mile along its eastern coast.

2. On the map, label the East Asian island country that has a population density of mostly 101–500 people per square mile.

3. Draw stars on the four countries on the map that have fewer than five people per square mile in most areas.

4. Circle the areas of China that have more than 500 people per square mile.

(continued)

© Harcourt

Name _____ Date _____

Directions Use the map on the previous page as well as an atlas to help you answer the questions that follow.

5 What is the population density for most of Saudi Arabia?

_____

6 Where are Saudi Arabia's densest regions located? _____

_____

_____

7 What are the four countries that have regions of more than 500 people per

square mile? _____

8 Where are the most densely populated regions in India located?

_____

_____

_____

_____

9 Which regions of India are the least densely populated? _____

_____

_____

10 Study both China and India on the map. Which country has larger regions with

more than 500 people per square mile? _____

_____

11 How are the population density patterns of China and India similar? How are they

different? _____

_____

_____

Use after reading Chapter 2, Skill Lesson, pages 58–59.

© Harcourt

Cultures and Societies

Directions Complete the puzzle by filling in the correct term for each definition below. Then unscramble the circled letters to help you find the word that will complete the paragraph below.

1 _ _ (_) _ _ (_) _ _ _ _

2 _ _ (_) _ _ _ _ _ _ _ _ (_) _

3 (_) _ _ _ _ _ _ _ _ _ _

4 (_) _ _ _ _ _ _ _ _

5 _ _ _ (_) _ _ _ _ _ (_) _ _

6 _ _ _ _ _ _ _ _ _ _ _

7 _ _ _ _ _ _ _ _ (_) _ _

8 (_) _ _ _ _ _ _ _ _ _

9 _ _ _ _ _ _ _ _ _ _ _ _ _ _

Terms

human society · ethnic group
enculturation · cultural diversity
cultural traits · cultural borrowing
assimilation · cultural diffusion
acculturation

Definitions

1. A group of people who share a culture and way of life are known by this name.
2. Only about ten percent of a society's cultural traits are its own because of this.
3. These are material or nonmaterial characteristics of a society's culture.
4. This is an organized group of people.
5. This happens when two societies have contact for a long time and exchange cultural traits.
6. This happens when immigrants give up their traditions and become part of their new country's culture.
7. This is the result when several ethnic groups live within the same country.
8. Learning national customs is an example of this process.
9. This happens when one society borrows cultural traits from another.

The Internet is the latest example of _____ that is spreading cultural traits around the world. At the beginning of the twenty-first century, the United States can be part of a great exchange of world cultures because it has so many computers connected to the Internet. Canada and the countries of Europe and East Asia also have a large presence on the Internet.

© Harcourt

Name _____ Date _____

Read Parallel Time Lines

Directions The parallel time line below shows the rise of civilization in three different areas of the world. Use the time lines to answer the questions on the next page.

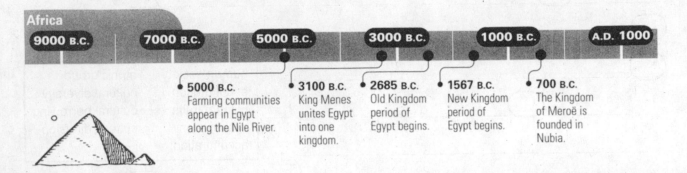

Africa

| 9000 B.C. | 7000 B.C. | 5000 B.C. | 3000 B.C. | 1000 B.C. | A.D. 1000 |

5000 B.C.
Farming communities appear in Egypt along the Nile River.

3100 B.C.
King Menes unites Egypt into one kingdom.

2685 B.C.
Old Kingdom period of Egypt begins.

1567 B.C.
New Kingdom period of Egypt begins.

700 B.C.
The Kingdom of Meroë is founded in Nubia.

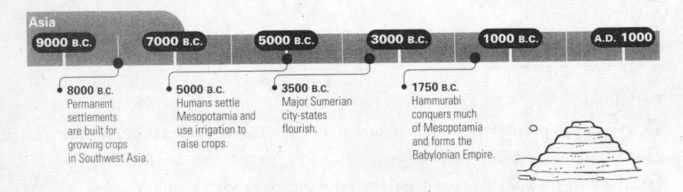

Asia

| 9000 B.C. | 7000 B.C. | 5000 B.C. | 3000 B.C. | 1000 B.C. | A.D. 1000 |

8000 B.C.
Permanent settlements are built for growing crops in Southwest Asia.

5000 B.C.
Humans settle Mesopotamia and use irrigation to raise crops.

3500 B.C.
Major Sumerian city-states flourish.

1750 B.C.
Hammurabi conquers much of Mesopotamia and forms the Babylonian Empire.

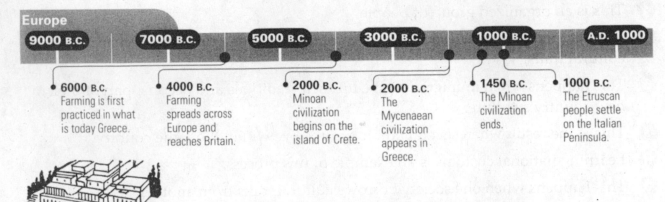

Europe

| 9000 B.C. | 7000 B.C. | 5000 B.C. | 3000 B.C. | 1000 B.C. | A.D. 1000 |

6000 B.C.
Farming is first practiced in what is today Greece.

4000 B.C.
Farming spreads across Europe and reaches Britain.

2000 B.C.
Minoan civilization begins on the island of Crete.

2000 B.C.
The Mycenaean civilization appears in Greece.

1450 B.C.
The Minoan civilization ends.

1000 B.C.
The Etruscan people settle on the Italian Peninsula.

© Harcourt

(continued)

Use after reading Chapter 2, Skill Lesson, pages 66–67.

Name _____ Date _____

1 Where and when was farming first practiced? _____
_____

2 When was farming first practiced in what is today Greece?
_____

3 How many years did it take from the time that farming began in what is today Greece for it to spread across Europe and reach Britain? _____
_____
_____

4 What happened around 5000 B.C. in Asia and Africa? _____
_____
_____

5 What civilizations began about 440 years before the New Kingdom period began in Egypt? _____
_____

6 Which country was first united about the same time that the Sumerian city-states flourished in Asia? _____

7 Which African kingdom was founded about 300 years after the Etruscans settled on the Italian Peninsula? _____

8 Which of these events happened first?
   The New Kingdom period began in Egypt.
   The Minoan civilization ended.
   Hammurabi established the Babylonian Empire.
_____
_____

Governments and Economies

Directions Study the diagram of the different kinds of industry. Use the diagram to help you answer the questions below.

1. Why is the trucking company a tertiary industry? _____

_____

_____

2. Which kind of industry is a cereal factory? _____

_____

3. What role does the supermarket have in the sale of the wheat?

_____

_____

_____

4. Does the diagram show the industries of a developed country or a developing

country? How do you know? _____

_____

_____

Use after reading Chapter 2, Lesson 3, pages 68–73.

© Harcourt

Name _____ Date _____

Looking at Regions

Directions Countries are political regions that can also be divided into smaller regions or subregions. In the United States these subregions are called states. The states can also be divided into smaller regions such as counties and townships. Create a map of the political regions of your home state by following the instructions below.

Draw a map of your state in the box, and label it.

Add major cities and towns to the map.

Find the location of your county in the state.

Draw and label the county.

Add important landforms and bodies of water to the map.

Draw and label an inset map of your city or town.

Locate and label important places related to the community's government.

Locate and label important industries in the community's economy.

© Harcourt

Name _____ Date _____

CITIZENSHIP SKILLS
Identify National Symbols

Directions Read the paragraph. Then match each flag to the description below. Write the letter of each flag on the line next to the correct description.

Flags are symbols of national identity. Flags can represent a country's people, geography, and culture. Many countries use symbols on their flags to link them to the past. Others use symbols that represent a religion, landforms, or industries found inside their borders. For example, the crescent moon with a star that is found on many flags is an important symbol of the religion of Islam. Some countries use color bars, such as red for courage, to describe their people.

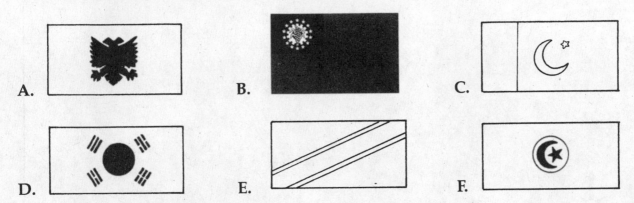

A. B. C.

D. E. F.

Descriptions

1 _____ Pakistan's flag has an important Islamic symbol and two colors representing the Muslim majority and the minority groups that live in that country.

2 _____ One symbol representing equality and four additional symbols representing the four seasons and compass directions are in the middle of the South Korean flag.

3 _____ Tanzania was formed when two countries, Zanzibar and Tanganyika, united. Tanzania's flag shows two equal pieces joined by a wide bar.

4 _____ A two-headed eagle sits in the center of Albania's flag, symbolizing this country's history as part of the Byzantine Empire.

5 _____ The crescent moon and star of Islam are placed in the center of the Tunisian flag.

6 _____ Myanmar's flag shows a machine wheel and a rice plant to represent industry and agriculture in that country.

Use after reading Chapter 2, Skill Lesson, pages 82–83.

© Harcourt

Name _____ Date _____

Patterns of Life

Directions Complete this graphic organizer to show that you understand how to make generalizations about patterns of settlement.

FACTS + DETAILS GENERALIZATION

People settle where the climate is mild and the soil is fertile. People also settle in cities to find work. Bodies of water are often near these places.

_____
_____
_____
_____
_____
_____
_____
_____

Differences in language, customs, and religion often separate cultures. Contact between cultures, however, spreads cultural ideas. Through technology, people of different cultures can more easily communicate with each other.

_____
_____
_____
_____
_____
_____
_____
_____

© Harcourt

Use after reading Chapter 2, pages 50–85.

2 Test Preparation

Directions Read each question and choose the best answer. Then fill in the circle for the answer you have chosen. Be sure to fill in the circle completely.

1 Choose the example of cultural assimilation.
- Ⓐ learning to speak a nation's official language
- Ⓑ practicing an ethnic tradition
- Ⓒ wearing traditional clothing
- Ⓓ forcing religious beliefs on other peoples

2 An example of human adaptation to the environment is—
- Ⓕ building a dam across a river.
- Ⓖ digging the Panama Canal.
- Ⓗ using natural resources to manufacture products.
- Ⓙ wearing heavy sweaters and clothing in a highland climate.

3 Which area has the least concentration of people?
- Ⓐ the Nile valley
- Ⓑ the Arctic Circle
- Ⓒ the Ganges River valley
- Ⓓ the Great European Plain

4 The term *majority rule* means that—
- Ⓕ a person seizes power and makes decisions for all the people.
- Ⓖ decisions are approved by a majority of the people before taking effect.
- Ⓗ a king or queen can make decisions for all the people.
- Ⓙ a group not chosen by the people makes the decisions.

5 Choose the example of a business in a secondary industry.
- Ⓐ a paper factory
- Ⓑ a hospital or doctor's office
- Ⓒ an architectural firm
- Ⓓ a logging company

© Harcourt

From Sea to Shining Sea

Directions A region is an area of land with parts that share common characteristics. The South is a region with many common characteristics such as landforms, climate, and products. Complete the crossword puzzle to learn some of the South's characteristics. Use your textbook to help you answer the questions below.

ACROSS

4 From June through November _____ strike the southern coast.

7 The South has many _____, such as the Everglades, which cover 4,000 square miles (about 10,000 sq km) of Florida.

8 The Northeast and the South regions share the _____ Mountains.

DOWN

1 The South is an _____ region because warm temperatures, long summers, and frequent rainfall make it easy to raise crops.

2 The _____ River is an important water highway for travel and trade in the region.

3 The warm climate of the South allows farmers to grow _____ such as oranges and limes.

5 The _____ Coastal Plain is a strip of land that begins in the Northeast and runs along the East and Gulf Coasts.

6 The South is a region of large cities. _____ is one of the large cities and is located in southeastern Texas.

© Harcourt

MAP AND GLOBE SKILLS

Read a Relief and Elevation Map

Directions Study the relief and elevation maps below. Use the maps to help you answer the questions that follow on page 29.

A **relief map** shows what kinds of land are located in a region using color or shading. A dark color shows high land, and lower, flatter land is shown with lighter colors. An **elevation map** measures the height of land from sea level. An elevation map uses patterns that connect all the areas that are the same height.

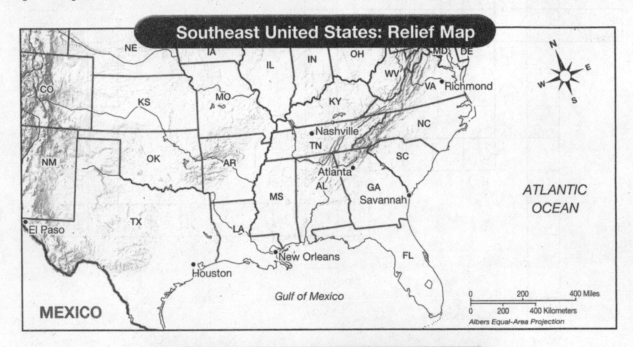

(continued)

© Harcourt

Use after reading Chapter 3, Skill Lesson, pages 104–105.

Name _____ Date _____

1 Study the relief map. Which city in Georgia is located on higher land, Savannah

or Atlanta? _____

2 Study the elevation map. Which two states are almost entirely at sea level?

_____

3 What is the highest elevation range in the state of North Carolina?

_____

4 Which city is located on higher land—Nashville, Tennessee, or Houston, Texas?

_____

Directions Use the maps on page 28 to identify the mystery states. Write the name of the correct state on the line that follows each clue.

5 This state has five areas of elevation. _____

6 Which state has the least land at or below 1,640 feet (305 m) above sea level?

_____

7 This is the state along the East Coast with the lowest relief.

_____

8 This state is on the East Coast and has three different areas of elevations that range

from sea level to 1,640 feet (305 m) above sea level. _____

_____

Name _____   Date _____

A New Republic

Directions Read the paragraph and the list of British laws that led to the
American Revolution. Then transport yourself back to 1775, and write a persuasive
letter to King George III. Try to persuade the British government to reverse its
laws, prevent violence, and grant the colonies representation in Parliament. Use
specific laws to make your argument.

In 1763 the French and Indian War ended, leaving Britain in control of almost all
of North America. The British Parliament decided that the 13 Colonies should pay for the
enormous expense of the war. Over the next ten years, Britain passed several laws that
taxed the colonists and restricted their freedom. Many colonists believed that there should
not be any laws passed without colonial representation in the British Parliament. Several
letters were sent by the colonists to the British government protesting the laws. The letters
were ignored. Only protests, violence, and revolution seemed to have any effect.

1764 Sugar Act: Taxed non-British goods entering the colonies.

1765 Quartering Act: Forced the colonies to provide housing for
British soldiers.

1765 Stamp Act: Taxed newspapers, almanacs, pamphlets, and other
documents.

1766 Declaratory Act: Stated how Parliament could pass any law for
the colonies.

1767 Townshend Acts: Taxed glass, lead, paint, paper, and tea.

1772 Tea Act: Cut the taxes on British tea, giving British Tea
merchants an unfair advantage over American merchants.

1774 Coercive Acts: Punished Massachusetts for the Boston Tea
Party by closing the port of Boston and seizing the colonial
government.

1775 New England Restraining Act: Prevented the New England
colonies from trading with any other place besides Britain.

© Harcourt

Name _____ Date _____

One People, Many Cultures

Directions Some consider jazz music to be the first original American art. Throughout the 20th century, many musicians experimented with jazz music. Read the biographies of two famous jazz musicians. Then answer the question below.

Duke Ellington (1899–1974)

Duke Ellington began playing the piano when he was six years old. Ellington did not like the piano and quit until he heard a form of jazz called ragtime. Ragtime was very different from the music that Ellington had studied as a child. He was so impressed by it that he taught himself to play this type of music. Soon Ellington was writing his own music and playing it at high school dances. In the 1920s, he moved to New York City and played with a band. Ellington became famous because his ragtime jazz was different from other artists' music. Ellington added African and Latin music to his arrangements. Over the next few decades, Ellington made records, toured the country, played on American radio shows, and made movies in Hollywood. In 1969, President Nixon awarded Duke Ellington the Presidential Medal of Freedom.

Ella Fitzgerald (1917–1996)

Ella Fitzgerald never had any formal training as a singer and became one of the world's greatest jazz vocalists. Fitzgerald was born in Newport News, Virginia, and by 1934 became a popular singer in New York City. Fitzgerald sang with a swing jazz band that played in many of New York's music clubs. At that time, discrimination made it difficult for African American musicians to perform. Fitzgerald's popularity helped open many doors for other African American musicians. Over the next four decades, she made hundreds of records and sang for many of the great jazz musicians, including Duke Ellington. Fitzgerald won many awards for her music, including 14 Grammy Awards.

What contributions did Ellington and Fitzgerald make to jazz music?

_____

_____

_____

_____

_____

© Harcourt

Name _____   Date _____

 READING SKILLS
Determine Point of View

Directions Read the statement below. Answer the questions that follow to determine the point of view of the statement's writer.

Editorials and Opinions

"The American West is a region under siege. It is an area threatened by overpopulation. In the last decade of the twentieth century, millions of Americans have moved to Montana, Idaho, Wyoming, Colorado, and the other states of the American West. In my opinion, the flood of people has been too much for the environment. As more people enter the region, animals are endangered. Entire species of animals are being threatened, as their habitats become new cities and towns. As communities grow, large amounts of forestland are destroyed. To prevent further damage, I believe that we need to put an immediate stop to migration to the American West."

George Smith,
director of the Preserve America's Nature organization

1 How does Mr. Smith feel about the migration of people to the American West?

_____

_____

2 Which words in Mr. Smith's statement help you to determine his point of view?

_____

_____

Directions Imagine that you have just read Mr. Smith's statement in a newspaper. Write a response to Mr. Smith that states an alternate point of view. Continue on another sheet of paper if you need more space.

_____

_____

_____

© Harcourt

Name _____   Date _____

Let Freedom Ring

Directions Study the responsibilities of the three branches of the United States government. Decide which branch performs each task. Write the letter of each task under the name of the correct branch name. Use your textbook or a copy of the United States Constitution to help you complete the diagram.

A. Enforces laws

B. Writes and passes laws

C. Decides if the actions of the executive branch are constitutional

D. Creates federal courts

E. Declares war on other countries

F. Leads our country's military

G. Appoints Supreme Court justices and ambassadors

H. Recommends laws

I. Decides if laws are constitutional

J. Approves appointments of Supreme Court justices and ambassadors

K. Amends the Constitution of the United States

L. Approves or vetoes laws

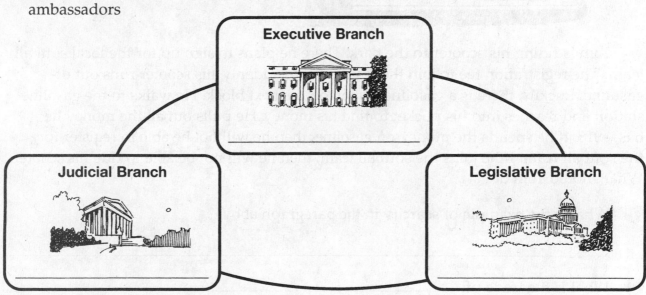

Executive Branch

Judicial Branch

Legislative Branch

Directions Read the question. Write your answer on the lines provided.

The Constitution of the United States places checks and balances on the power of each of the three branches of government. What are two examples of the checks and balances?

_____

_____

_____

_____

© Harcourt

Name _____   Date _____

CITIZENSHIP SKILLS
Make Economic Choices

Directions Making economic choices can be difficult. Scarcity forces us to make trade-offs—giving up one item to get another. Read the paragraph below. Then answer the questions to help Tom make a difficult economic decision.

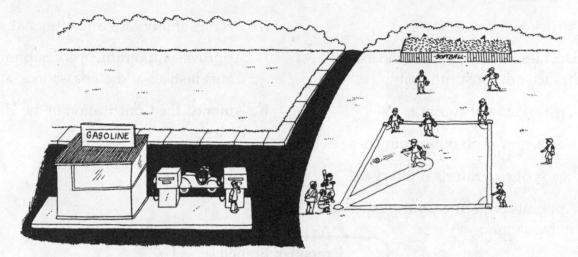

Tom is riding his scooter to the park. There he plans to sign up for the local softball team. The registration fee to join the team is $15. Suddenly, his scooter runs out of gasoline. Luckily, there is a gasoline station on the next block. He walks to the gasoline station and reaches into his pocket to find his money. He pulls out all the money he has—$15. If he spends the money on gasoline, then he will not be able to register for the softball team. If he joins the softball team, then he will not be able to ride his scooter. What should Tom do?

1 What is the example of scarcity in the paragraph above?

_____

2 What is the trade-off? _____

_____

3 If Tom chooses to buy gasoline for the scooter, what is the opportunity cost of his

economic decision? _____

4 What choice would you make? Explain whether you would buy gasoline or join the

softball team. _____

_____

© Harcourt

The United States

Directions Complete this graphic organizer to show that you understand how to summarize key points about the United States.

KEY POINTS → SUMMARY

LESSON 1: KEY POINTS	LESSON 1: SUMMARY

LESSON 2: KEY POINTS	LESSON 2: SUMMARY

LESSON 3: KEY POINTS	LESSON 3: SUMMARY

LESSON 4: KEY POINTS	LESSON 4: SUMMARY

© Harcourt

Use after reading Chapter 3, pages 96–131.

3

Name _____   Date _____

Test Preparation

1 Which of these regions of the United States is the smallest in area but not population?

Ⓐ the South

Ⓑ the West

Ⓒ the Northeast

Ⓓ the Middle West

2 Why do most people in the Northeast live east of the Appalachian Mountains?

Ⓕ West of the mountains are large plateaus.

Ⓖ The mountains formed a natural barrier to settlers' westward movement.

Ⓗ The Pacific coastal plain is very narrow and has few harbors.

Ⓙ The South had many water-filled swamps that slowed settlers' movements.

3 Which of these statements describes a republic?

Ⓐ The government has three parts that include executive, judicial, and legislative branches.

Ⓑ All the citizens of the country participate in making and enforcing laws.

Ⓒ A king or queen leads the country and makes all laws.

Ⓓ The voters choose representatives who make and enforce the laws for them.

4 The federal and state governments share—

Ⓕ the power to establish an education system.

Ⓖ the power to form relations with other countries.

Ⓗ the power to make laws.

Ⓙ the power to make and distribute money.

5 Which statement is an example of a positive social change in recent United States history?

Ⓐ Immigrants came to the United States and often remained in cities.

Ⓑ Americans looked to Europe for trends in art, music, and architecture.

Ⓒ Today more women and minorities work in jobs and hold political offices.

Ⓓ Many Americans faced discrimination and could not own property or vote.

© Harcourt

Use after reading Chapter 3, pages 96–131.

Land and the People

Directions Read about one problem facing the Canadian people. Then answer the questions that follow.

Who Can Fish?

Before the arrival of the Europeans, Native Canadians in the Atlantic Provinces and Quebec fished in what are today the waters of the North Atlantic. The Native Canadian fishers harvested lobsters, cod, and other seafood to survive. With the arrival of the Europeans, fishing became an important industry in eastern Canada. Large companies or commercial fisheries harvested millions of tons of fish over the years. In fact so many fish had been harvested by the late twentieth century that the Canadian government declared the region overfished. The government then passed laws to limit the amount of seafood that could be harvested.

Since the Canadian government's decision to limit fishing, many people in Canada have been affected. Both the Native Canadians and people of European descent who depend on fishing have lost income. Some of the Native Canadians in the region believe that the laws of the Canadian government do not apply to them. They claim that treaties signed by their nations and Canada long ago allow them to continue fishing. Many Native Canadians continue to fish the waters of the North Atlantic. Several people have been arrested for fishing and put on trial by the government.

In 1999 one trial went all the way to Canada's Supreme Court. Canada's highest court ruled that the 34 Native Canadian nations could still fish when and where they wanted. Many Canadians disagreed, and violence broke out. Some Native Canadians found their fishing equipment vandalized. Others were arrested by the Canadian government for overfishing because the laws were not changed.

Fishing is an important industry to the people of Canada. Both Native Canadians and European Canadians in the Atlantic Provinces depend upon it for their livelihood. The Native Canadian nations believe that it is their right to fish as much as they want. Others worry that these nations will overfish the region and destroy the future of the fishing industry.

(continued)

Name _____ Date _____

Canadian police officer	Canadian Supreme Court judge
European Canadian fisher	Native Canadian fisher

1 "My people have been fishing in the waters of the North Atlantic for generations. Long before the Europeans arrived, the cod and other seafood gave life to my people. My people cannot be held responsible for overfishing the region and should not be punished for it."

_____

2 "We have laws in Canada and right now the law states that people can practice only limited fishing. The law applies to everyone. So until that law is changed, we will have to arrest anyone, Native Canadian or European Canadian, who is overfishing in restricted waters."

_____

3 "The Supreme Court is giving some Canadians an unfair advantage over others. My community needs to fish and make a living just as those 34 Native Canadian nations. It is unjust that some Canadians be allowed to continue fishing while my community and many more are denied that same right. Besides, if the people of Canada are supposed to be conserving the fish supply, then letting some groups continue fishing will not solve this problem."

_____

4 "The law of Canada above all should be fair—for all Canadians. Throughout history, the government of Canada has signed treaties in good faith with the Native Canadian nations. Our recent fishing laws did not maintain the special relationships we had with the Native Canadians. Our recent fishing laws should not change the rights that Canada granted the Native Canadian nations in earlier treaties. These nations do still have the right to fish in the waters of the North Atlantic."

_____

5 What do you think about the Canadian fishing crisis in the Atlantic Provinces? Write your opinions in a short paragraph below. You may use a separate sheet of paper.

_____

_____

_____

© Harcourt

Use after reading Chapter 4, Lesson 1, pages 134–141.

Name _____   Date _____

Through the Centuries

Directions Below are products of two different early groups that settled in Canada. Read each description, and study the drawings. Use the drawings to answer the questions and describe the groups that made these products.

Canada's first people were the Native Canadians who crossed a land bridge from Asia sometime between 12,000 and 40,000 years ago. Some settled in the deep forests of the southeast and the west coast. Others settled the rocky Canadian Shield, the cold northern territories, and the flat, treeless Interior Plains. The Native Canadians used whatever resources the regions had to offer in order to survive. We can study the products they left behind to learn about the regions they lived in and how they used resources to survive.

Assiniboine tepee, shoe, and tool made from the American bison

Nootka canoe, tool, and house made from many resources

1 What do the Assiniboine products show about the region of Canada in which

that group lived? _____

_____

_____

2 What do the Assiniboine products show about that group and how it used

natural resources? _____

_____

_____

_____

3 In what type of region did the Nootka people live? How did the Nootka use the

resources of its region to survive? _____

_____

_____

_____

© Harcourt

Canada's Government

Directions Hold an election to set up a classroom government that is based on the Canadian parliamentary system. Study the chart below and carefully read the instructions. Follow each step to elect your class leaders.

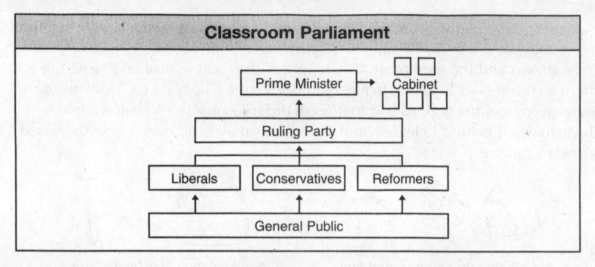

Classroom Parliament

1. As a class, divide into four groups: Liberals, Conservatives, Reformers, and general public. The members of the three political parties are all candidates for the position of Member of Parliament, or MP.

2. Everyone should vote for one candidate. Fill in the name of your candidate on a piece of paper and pass your ballot to your teacher.

3. Tally the votes and announce the names of the candidates who received votes. All the candidates who received votes have seats in the classroom Parliament.

4. Total each political party's MPs. The party with the most elected MPs controls the classroom Parliament as the ruling party.

5. The MPs of the ruling party should choose a leader, or a prime minister. The prime minister must choose five cabinet members to advise him or her about classroom laws. The prime minister can only choose the ministers from the elected MPs.

Directions Answer the question below. Write your answer on the lines provided.

6. Describe two ways that a parliamentary election is different from an election in the

United States. _____

_____

_____

_____

CHART AND GRAPH SKILLS
Follow a Flow Chart

Directions Study the flow chart. Then use the information in the flow chart to answer the questions on the following page.

The School Budget Process

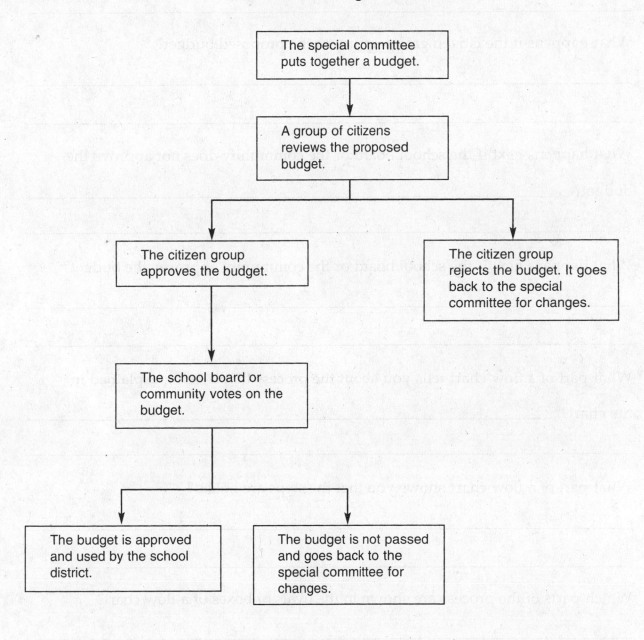

The special committee puts together a budget.

A group of citizens reviews the proposed budget.

The citizen group approves the budget.

The citizen group rejects the budget. It goes back to the special committee for changes.

The school board or community votes on the budget.

The budget is approved and used by the school district.

The budget is not passed and goes back to the special committee for changes.

© Harcourt

(continued)

Name _____ Date _____

Directions Study the flow chart on page 41 and use it to help you answer the questions below.

1 What is the process that is being explained on page 41?

_____

2 Which group is the first to review the special committee's proposed budget?

_____

3 What happens if the citizen group approves the proposed budget?

_____

_____

4 What happens next if the school board or the community does not approve the

budget? _____

_____

5 What happens next if the school board or the community approves the budget?

_____

_____

6 What part of a flow chart tells you about the process that is being explained in

the chart? _____

_____

7 What part of a flow chart shows you that the steps are linked?

_____

_____

8 Which parts of the process are shown in the ovals or boxes of a flow chart?

_____

_____

Use after reading Chapter 4, Skill Lesson, pages 154–155.

Name _____ Date _____

Canada

Directions Complete this graphic organizer to show that you understand how to draw conclusions about Canada based on what you read and what you already know.

WHAT YOU READ ➕ WHAT YOU KNOW → CONCLUSION

People living in Canada have settled in places with fertile soil and access to water. They use natural resources from northern Canada but live in the south where the climate is warmer.

➕

→

➕ Every country has its own form of government. The government of the United States is a democracy. People elect officials and no one branch of government has absolute power.

→

Name _____   Date _____

4 Test Preparation

Directions Read each question and choose the best answer. Then fill in the circle for the answer you have chosen. Be sure to fill in the circle completely.

1 Which region has frozen soil, ice, and is the least likely to provide Canadians with fertile farmland?
- Ⓐ Appalachian region
- Ⓑ Arctic Islands region
- Ⓒ St. Lawrence Lowlands region
- Ⓓ Interior Plains region

2 In the Canadian government, the official with the smallest role is—
- Ⓕ the Speaker of the House of Commons.
- Ⓖ the prime minister.
- Ⓗ the king or queen of Britain.
- Ⓙ a Member of Parliament.

3 Unlike the President of the United States, the Canadian prime minister is not chosen by the people. He or she is—
- Ⓐ selected by the king or queen of Britain.
- Ⓑ chosen by the MPs of the ruling party.
- Ⓒ elected by the Supreme Court.
- Ⓓ chosen by the leaders of the provinces.

4 Which Native Canadian group survived by creating products from the American bison?
- Ⓕ Ottawa
- Ⓖ Huron
- Ⓗ Inuit
- Ⓙ Assiniboine

5 What was the effect of Giovanni Caboto's search for a northern water route to Asia?
- Ⓐ The English claimed the land of Newfoundland.
- Ⓑ The English claimed all the land around the St. Lawrence River.
- Ⓒ The Vikings explored Canada but returned to Scandinavia.
- Ⓓ The French founded the colony of New France.

© Harcourt

Use after reading Chapter 4, pages 132–157.

Name _____ Date _____

A Rugged Land

Directions Mexico is a land of steep mountains, hot deserts, and high plateaus. It also has three climate and vegetation regions: the tierra caliente, the tierra templada, and the tierra fría. Study the cross-section of this rugged land. Use the cross-section to answer the questions that follow.

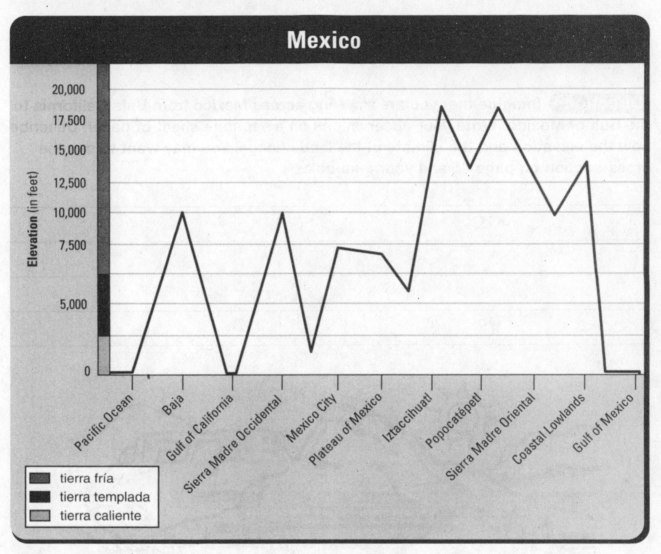

1 Into which climate and vegetation zone does the volcano Popocatépetl reach?

_____

2 What is the average height of the Plateau of Mexico? _____

3 Into which climate and vegetation zone does the land next to the Gulf of Mexico

fall? _____

4 At how many feet above sea level is Mexico City located? _____

(continued)

© Harcourt

Name _____ Date _____

Directions Below are the names of six cities, landforms, and bodies of water found in Mexico. Number them 1–6 in the correct order of elevation, using 1 for the lowest and 6 for the highest feature. Use the cross-section on page 45 to help you complete the activity.

_____ Mexico City   _____ Plateau of Mexico

_____ Iztaccíhuatl   _____ Sierra Madre Oriental

_____ Gulf of California   _____ Sierra Madre Occidental

Directions Imagine that you are traveling across Mexico from Baja California to the Gulf of Mexico. Write your observations on a separate sheet of paper. Describe how the elevation and the climate of the land change. You may want to use the cross-section on page 45 and your textbook.

_____

_____

_____

_____

_____

_____

© Harcourt

Use after reading Chapter 5, Lesson 1, pages 172–176.

Creating a Mexican Culture

Directions Read the following paragraphs about the city of Tenochtitlán. Then number the illustrations to show the order of events in the city's growth.

The capital of the Aztec Empire was a fabulous city called Tenochtitlán. Although the settlement eventually became one of Earth's largest cities, it had very simple beginnings. In 1325 the Aztecs came to the Valley of Mexico and claimed an island in the middle of Lake Texcoco. The island had poor soil, and few crops could grow there. To solve this problem, the Aztecs built floating gardens called *chinampas* on the lake.

The Aztecs built these floating gardens by first making large rafts from the reeds that grew along the lake. The rafts were covered with many layers of mud and were anchored to the lake floor with large poles. Then seeds were planted in the layers of mud. As the plants grew, their roots reached down into the lake water. On some rafts, the Aztecs planted willow trees to hold the soil and keep it from blowing or washing away.

The Aztec harvests were plentiful, and the floating gardens grew larger. The Aztecs then began to fill in the spaces between the chinampas in the same way. There they built homes, shops, and temples. Eventually, the settlement grew to include other small islands in Lake Texcoco. Large causeways were built to connect the growing city to the mainland and the other islands. Later the Aztecs would extend their rule to areas beyond Lake Texcoco, but the city of Tenochtitlán would always remain the empire's largest and most powerful city.

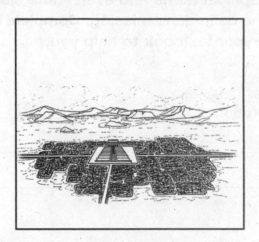

_____

_____

_____

Use after reading Chapter 5, Lesson 2, pages 177–182.

Yesterday and Today

Directions A glossary is a list of specialized words and their definitions. It is found in many of the books you read. Sometimes a glossary includes historical or geographical terms and even some biographical information. Below is a glossary with the definitions missing. Complete it by filling in the definitions. You may want to use your textbook to help you.

C

Constitution of 1917 _____

_____

_____

D

Díaz, Porfirio _____

_____

F

Federal District _____

_____

G

General Congress _____

_____

H

Hidalgo, Miguel _____

_____

I

Institutional Revolutionary Party _____

_____

J

Juá rez, Benito _____

_____

Use after reading Chapter 5, Lesson 3, pages 183–187.

© Harcourt

READING SKILLS
Identify Cause and Effect

Directions Read the paragraphs below about Benito Juárez, the Mexican War of Reform, and Maximilian, the Austrian prince who became Mexico's emperor. Then use the information in the paragraphs to complete the activities on page 50.

In 1857 a group of Mexicans known as the Liberals took control of the Mexican government. They estabished a new constitution, limited the president's power and that of the Catholic Church, and set up regular elections. Many Mexicans in the army and in the Catholic Church, as well as wealthy landowners, were not happy with these changes. They decided to overthrow the government, forcing the Mexican president and his cabinet to flee.

Benito Juárez, the Chief Justice of the Supreme Court, decided to resist. He declared himself President of Mexico and set up his capital at Veracruz. As a result the civil war known as the War of Reform began. By 1861 Juárez's army had seized Mexico City. In 1862 France, Britain, and Spain sent military forces to Mexico to secure repayment of debts from Juárez's government. They soon occupied the port of Veracruz.

Maximilian 1832–1867

The French, however, had another plan. The French Emperor Napoleon III wanted to set up a new French Empire in Mexico. He sent a large army to Mexico, marched to Mexico City, and seized the capital. Then Napoleon placed an Austrian prince named Maximilian on the throne of Mexico.

Maximilian became the Emperor of Mexico in 1864, but only a few Mexicans recognized his rule. Most saw the French forces as invaders and Maximilian as a puppet ruler. Juárez and his army continued to fight the French. After years of fighting, Napoleon decided to pull the French army out of Mexico in 1867. Without the French to protect him, Maximilian was captured in a battle at the town of Querétaro. Soon after, Maximilian was put on trial, found guilty of treason, and executed. Juárez's army quickly retook control of Mexico City and the entire country.

© Harcourt

(continued)

Name _____ Date _____

Directions Study the diagram below. Fill in the missing causes and effects with information from the story of the War of Reform on page 49.

CAUSES EFFECTS

The Mexican president and cabinet flee when the government is overthrown. _____
_____
_____

_____
_____
_____ → The governments of France, Britain, and Spain fear that Juárez's government will not repay its debts.

The French send an army to Mexico and take control of Mexico City. → _____
_____
_____

_____
_____
_____ → Juárez captures Maximilian and takes control of Mexico.

© Harcourt

Use after reading Chapter 5, Skill Lesson, pages 188–189.

Name _____ Date _____

Mexico

Directions Complete this graphic organizer to show that you understand how to compare and contrast different groups and cultures, such as the Olmecs and the Maya.

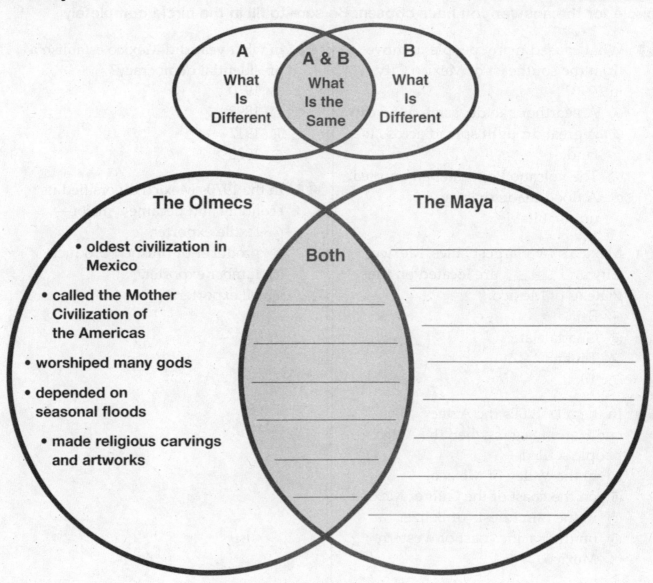

A
What Is Different

A & B
What Is the Same

B
What Is Different

The Olmecs

- oldest civilization in Mexico
- called the Mother Civilization of the Americas
- worshiped many gods
- depended on seasonal floods
- made religious carvings and artworks

Both

_____

_____

_____

_____

_____

The Maya

_____

_____

_____

_____

_____

_____

_____

_____

© Harcourt

Name _____ Date _____

5 Test Preparation

Directions Read each question and choose the best answer. Then fill in the circle for the answer you have chosen. Be sure to fill in the circle completely.

1 What caused many people to move from the southeast of Mexico City in 1996?
- Ⓐ An earthquake devastated the city.
- Ⓑ A great drought spread across the land.
- Ⓒ The volcano Popocatépetl erupted.
- Ⓓ A flood made the city uninhabitable.

2 Mexico's two largest cities, Mexico City and _____, are located on the Plateau of Mexico.
- Ⓕ Baja
- Ⓖ Guadalajara
- Ⓗ Tijuana
- Ⓙ Tikal

3 In the A.D. 1200s the Aztec civilization began when the Aztec people settled—
- Ⓐ in the Valley of Mexico.
- Ⓑ on the coast of the Gulf of Mexico.
- Ⓒ in the rain forests of Belize.
- Ⓓ on the Pacific coast of western Mexico.

4 In what year did Mexico establish a presidential democracy?
- Ⓕ 1910
- Ⓖ 1898
- Ⓗ 1917
- Ⓙ 1922

5 In the 1970s Mexico diversified its economy and became a major—
- Ⓐ textile exporter.
- Ⓑ producer of finished products.
- Ⓒ lumber exporter.
- Ⓓ oil exporter.

© Harcourt

Use after reading Chapter 5, pages 170–191.

Mountains, Volcanoes, Islands, and Hurricanes

Directions Middle America has many special geographical features, such as cays, straits, and forests. Study the terms in the box below. Some are terms you learned in your textbook. Others you learned before. Label each of the pictures below with one of the terms from the box.

archipelago	cay	coastal lowland	coniferous trees	coral reef
isthmus	peninsula	strait	trade winds	volcano

1  _____

2 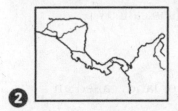 _____

3 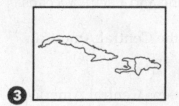 _____

4  _____

5  _____

6  _____

7  _____

8  _____

9  _____

10 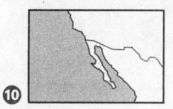 _____

(continued)

© Harcourt

Name _____ Date _____

11 The two subregions that make up Middle America are

_____ and the Caribbean.

12 A _____ is a small, low-lying island made of sand, limestone, or coral.

13 In the mountainous areas of Central America, there are many cone-bearing

evergreen trees called _____.

14 Winds that consistently blow from northeast of the Caribbean toward the equator

are called the _____.

15 The chain of islands in the Caribbean is an _____.

16 A hard, stony material made from the skeletons of sea animals is called

_____.

17 At the southernmost tip of Central America is a narrow strip of land, called an

_____, that separates the Atlantic and Pacific Oceans.

18 The _____ areas located along the Central American coast have a tropical climate with plenty of rain.

19 The ash from erupting _____ keeps Central America's soil fertile.

20 Cuba is the largest _____ in the Caribbean archipelago.

Use after reading Chapter 6, Lesson 1, pages 194–199.

© Harcourt

Influences of the Past

Directions Many ethnic groups settled in Central America and the Caribbean. Read each of the descriptions below. Draw lines connecting the group descriptions and the correct group names below. There may be more than one line from a description or to a group.

1 Scientists believe this group was the first to settle on the Caribbean islands.

Arawaks

Ciboneys

2 These three different ethnic groups lived in the Caribbean region during the 1300s and the 1400s.

Caribs

English

3 These colonists began settling on the islands of the Caribbean in the early 1600s.

French

4 The people of this civilization built more than 100 cities in present-day Belize, El Salvador, Guatemala, and Honduras.

Dutch

Maya

5 This group of colonists forced the Arawaks to work as slaves on large plantations.

Spanish

Directions On a separate sheet of paper, write a short paragraph that explains how the Dutch, English, French, and Spanish influenced the people that lived in the region.

_____

_____

(continued)

Name _____ Date _____

6 _____ In 1492, Christopher Columbus, an explorer sailing for France, landed in the Bahamas.

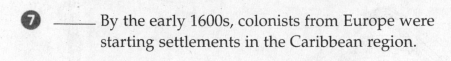

_____

_____

7 _____ By the early 1600s, colonists from Europe were starting settlements in the Caribbean region.

_____

_____

8 _____ The English and the French did not get their plantation workers from the

African slave trade. _____

_____

9 _____ As sugar production in the Caribbean grew in the 1700s, so did the number of

Africans in the Caribbean population. _____

_____

10 _____ In some places in the Caribbean region, slavery was abolished because the

price of tobacco fell. _____

_____

11 _____ The Aztecs built more than 100 cities in what are today Belize,

El Salvador, Guatemala, and Honduras. _____

_____

12 _____ The Spanish arrived in Central America in the 1700s.

_____

_____

© Harcourt

Use after reading Chapter 6, Lesson 2, pages 200–205.

Name _____   Date _____

Contrasts in Governing

Directions Read the descriptions of political events below and write the date when each event occurred. Then write the number of the event in the correct place under the time line below. You may want to use your textbook to help you figure out the correct dates.

1 _____ The Central American countries form a federation called the United Provinces of Central America.

2 _____ Panama wins independence from Colombia.

3 _____ Oscar Arias Sanchez wins the Nobel Peace Prize for creating a Central American peace plan.

4 _____ Costa Rica, El Salvador, Guatemala, Honduras, and Nicaragua win independence from Spain.

5 _____ Belize becomes an independent country.

6 _____ Haiti wins independence from France.

7 _____ The United States purchases the Virgin Islands from Denmark.

8 _____ Fidel Castro and his supporters create a Communist government in Cuba.

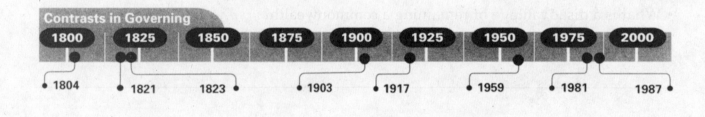

Contrasts in Governing

1800	1825	1850	1875	1900	1925	1950	1975	2000

1804   1821   1823   1903   1917   1959   1981   1987

_____   _____   _____   _____

© Harcourt

Name _____   Date _____

CITIZENSHIP SKILLS
Make a Thoughtful Decision

Directions Imagine you are a citizen
of Puerto Rico preparing to vote on
whether the island should remain a
commonwealth or become the 51st
state of the United States. Read the
paragraph below. Then make a thoughtful decision by writing a brief paragraph
to answer the questions that follow.

The U.S. and Puerto Rico

    In 1952, the people of Puerto Rico
adopted a constitution that created the
Commonwealth of Puerto Rico. As
inhabitants of a United States territory
Puerto Ricans are citizens of the United
States and share most of the rights of other
United States citizens. For example, the
people of Puerto Rico cannot vote for the President or members of Congress and have
little say in the creation of the country's national laws. On the positive side, citizens of
Puerto Rico maintain their heritage and do not pay federal income taxes.

• What is an advantage of remaining a commonwealth?

• What is a disadvantage of remaining a commonwealth?

• Will you vote for Puerto Rico to become a state? Why?

_____

_____

_____

_____

_____

_____

_____

© Harcourt

Central America and the Caribbean

Directions Complete the graphic organizer below to show that you understand the sequence of events that ended Spanish control of Central America and led to the creation of independent countries there. Complete the next organizer to show that you understand the order of events that caused enslaved Africans to be brought to the Caribbean.

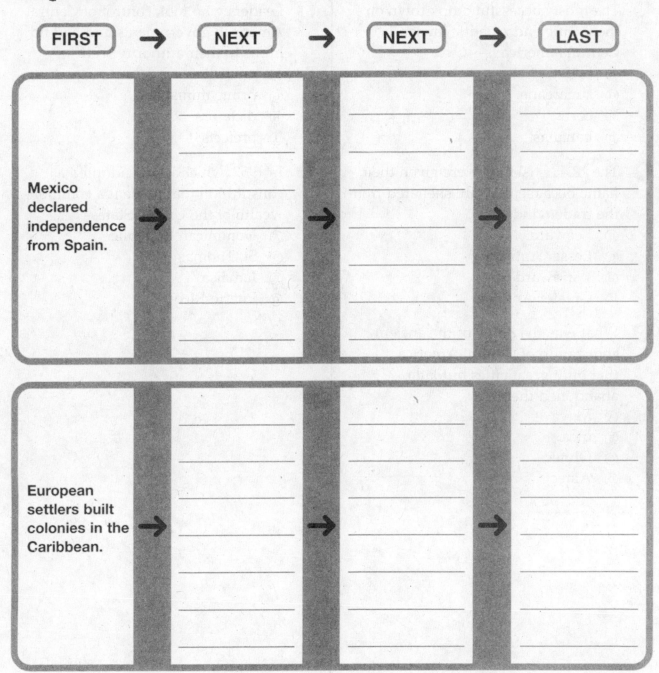

FIRST → NEXT → NEXT → LAST

Mexico declared independence from Spain.

European settlers built colonies in the Caribbean.

© Harcourt

Name _____ Date _____

6 Test Preparation

Directions Read each question and choose the best answer. Then fill in the circle for the answer you have chosen. Be sure to fill in the circle completely.

1. The most successful crop grown on the Pacific and Atlantic lowlands of Central America is—
   - Ⓐ coffee.
   - Ⓑ sugarcane.
   - Ⓒ corn.
   - Ⓓ bananas.

2. The _____ Islands were given their name because they are sheltered from the trade winds.
   - Ⓕ Leeward
   - Ⓖ Lesser Antilles
   - Ⓗ Windward
   - Ⓙ Greater Antilles

3. What was the name of the ancient civilization of Central America that built great cities but later abandoned them?
   - Ⓐ Maya
   - Ⓑ Inca
   - Ⓒ Olmec
   - Ⓓ Aztec

4. Leaders who took control of Central American governments and had no limits to their authority were—
   - Ⓕ guerrillas.
   - Ⓖ prime ministers.
   - Ⓗ dictators.
   - Ⓙ prefects.

5. In 1952, which island adopted a constitution that made it a commonwealth of the United States?
   - Ⓐ Dominican Republic
   - Ⓑ St. Thomas
   - Ⓒ Jamaica
   - Ⓓ Puerto Rico

© Harcourt

Use after reading Chapter 6, pages 192–217.

A Vast Land

Directions Gillian just returned from her vacation in South America. Below is a letter she wrote to a friend about some of the continent's special physical features. After Gillian mailed the letter, rain washed off some of the ink. To help Karla read the letter, fill in missing names.

January 23

Dear Karla:

   I had an amazing time in South America. I visited many cities. I also saw many beautiful landforms and bodies of water.

   The **1** _____ River is part of the largest river system in the world. That was what I saw first. I did not have the chance to see the Río de la Plata, which consists of the

Paraná, Paraguay, and **2** _____ Rivers. I did learn that the Río de la Plata is not a river at all. It is an estuary, or the mouth of a river into which the ocean tide flows.

   Next I traveled to the **3** _____. This area north of the Amazon River is mainly grasslands with scattered trees. Later I traveled south into the Andes Mountains. They stretch 4,500 miles from

4 _____ to the southern tip of South America. From the Andes I crossed the Central Plains to visit the Gran Chaco. This large region of scrub forests covers parts of Argentina, Paraguay, and

5 _____. I did not have the chance to see the other three areas of the Central Plains called the Llanos, the Selva, and

the **6** _____.

   Before leaving South America, I went to the **7** _____ Desert in northern Chile. It is one of the driest regions on Earth. Traveling south, I found myself in the part of South America closest to Antarctica. It's called

the **8** _____.

   I wish you could see this beautiful continent.

Your friend,

Gillian

(continued)

Name _____ Date _____

Directions While Gillian was in South America, she drew pictures of many different products that are produced there. But Gillian did not write down the countries in which she found them. Write the names of the products next to the countries where they are produced. Some can be matched with more than one country. Use your textbook to help you complete the activity.

Argentina

_____

_____

_____

_____

_____

_____

Bananas

Computers

Beef

Brazil

_____

_____

_____

_____

Grains

Airplanes

Venezuela

Consumer Goods

_____

_____

Petroleum

Chile

Coffee

Automobiles

_____

_____

© Harcourt

Use after reading Chapter 7, Lesson 1, pages 220–227.

MAP AND GLOBE SKILLS
Read a Map of Cultural Regions

Directions Cultural maps use symbols or colors to display information about the people living in a region. Use the cultural map of Brazil below to answer the questions on page 64.

Language Regions of Brazil

Boa Vista
RORAIMA
AMAPÁ
AMAZONAS
PARÁ
MARANHÃO
CEARÁ
RIO GRANDE DO NORTE
PIAUÍ
PARAÍBA
PERNAMBUCO
ACRE
Rio Branco
TOCANTINS
ALAGOAS
RONDÔNIA
MATO GROSSO
BAHIA
SERGIPE
Salvador
GOIÁS
Brasília
FEDERAL DIST.
MINAS GERAIS
ESPÍRITO SANTO
MATO GROSSO DO SUL
SÃO PAULO
RIO DE JANEIRO
PARANÁ
Rio de Janeiro
São Paulo
SANTA CATARINA
RIO GRANDE DO SUL

Portuguese-speaking area
Native American language area

© Harcourt

(continued)

Name _____ Date _____

Directions Use the map of Brazil on page 63 to answer the following questions.

① What is the purpose of this map? _____

_____

_____

② Which languages are spoken in Brazil? _____

_____

③ Which language is spoken in the city of São Paulo? _____

④ Which language is spoken in most of Brazil's coastal regions?

_____

⑤ Which languages are spoken in the Brazilian state of Acre?

_____

⑥ Which state is farthest south and has citizens who speak both Portuguese and

Native American languages? _____

⑦ Which language is spoken in most of Bahia? _____

⑧ Which language is more widely spoken in the state of Roraima: Portuguese or

a Native American language? _____

⑨ In which of the following states are both Portuguese and Native American
languages spoken: Sergipe, Mato Grosso, Rio Grande do Sul, or Pernambuco?

_____

Use after reading Chapter 7, Skill Lesson, pages 228–229.

© Harcourt

Name _____ Date _____

Cultures and Lifeways

Directions Explore the ruins of the Inca city of Machu Picchu. At the site, you will find several signs with information about the Incas and their empire. Each sign is missing important information. Complete each sign by writing short statements about the topic. Use your textbook to help you complete the activity.

Sample: Inca Government

The Incas were ruled by an emperor. The emperor forced the peoples

the Incas conquered to follow the Inca way of life.

Adapting to the Land

_____

_____

Types of Crops

_____

_____

Language

_____

_____

© Harcourt

CHART AND GRAPH SKILLS
Read a Double-Bar Graph

Directions Double-bar graphs present two sets of statistics so that they can easily be compared. Study the graphs below, and use them to answer the questions on page 67.

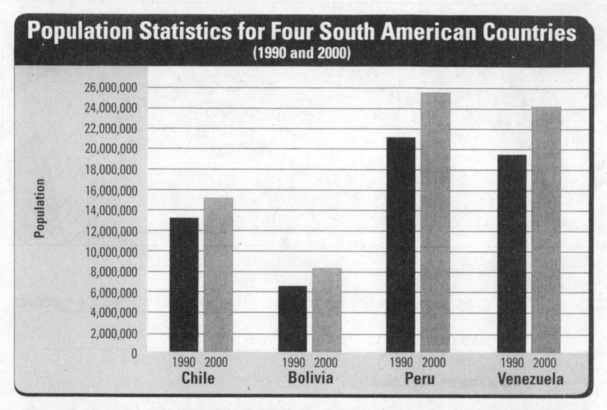

Population Statistics for Four South American Countries
(1990 and 2000)

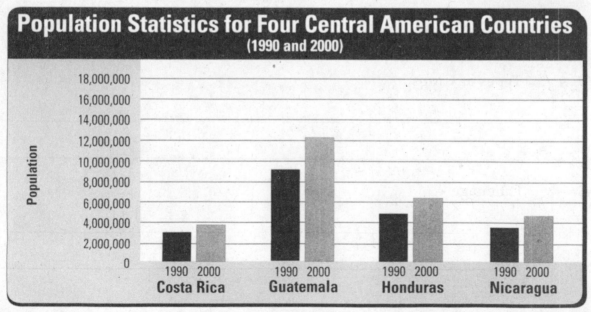

Population Statistics for Four Central American Countries
(1990 and 2000)

(continued)

© Harcourt

Name _____ Date _____

1 What information is being compared in each of the double-bar graphs?

_____

2 Study the population statistics for Chile, Bolivia, Nicaragua, and Honduras. Which country had the largest population in both 1990 and 2000?

_____

3 Study the population statistics for Bolivia, Nicaragua, and Honduras. Which country experienced the smallest population growth between 1990 and 2000?

_____

4 Do the graphs show that any country experienced a decline in population

between 1990 and 2000? _____

5 Which South American country had the largest population in both 1990

and 2000? _____

6 Which Central American countries had smaller populations than Bolivia in both

1990 and 2000? _____

7 List the South American and Central American countries that experienced a population growth of 3 or more million people between 1990 and 2000.

_____

8 Which South American and Central American countries experienced a population growth of about 2 million people between 1990 and 2000?

_____

9 Which four countries had the largest populations in the year 2000? List them in

order, largest to smallest. _____

_____

10 Which country had the smallest population in both 1990 and 2000?

_____

Building a Future

Directions Simón Bolívar and José de San Martín were freedom fighters who played a major role in bringing independence to much of South America. Read the list of South American countries below. Sort the countries into those freed by Bolívar and those freed by San Martín. Then write each country's name next to the picture of the freedom fighter who helped that country gain its independence.

Argentina	Bolivia	Brazil	Chile	Colombia
Ecuador	Paraguay	Peru	Venezuela	

_____
_____
_____
_____

Simón Bolívar   _____

_____
_____
_____
_____

José de San Martín   _____

Directions Write a short paragraph to answer the following question. You may want to use your textbook to help you complete the activity.

Two South American countries listed above were not freed by Bolívar or San Martín. Name the countries, and describe how each gained its independence.

_____

_____

_____

_____

_____

_____

_____

© Harcourt

Name _____ Date _____

South America

Directions Complete these graphic organizers to show that, by combining what you read with what you already know, you can make inferences about cultural influences in South America.

$$\boxed{\text{DETAILS + KNOWLEDGE}} \rightarrow \boxed{\text{INFERENCE}}$$

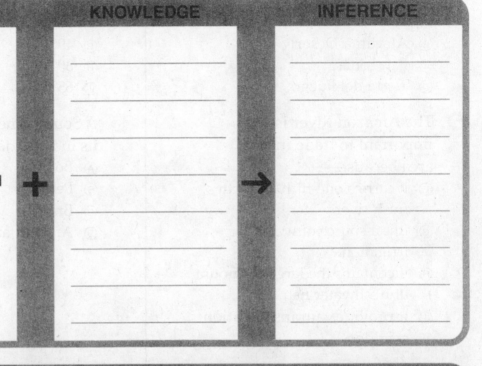

DETAILS	KNOWLEDGE	INFERENCE
The Incas settled in Peru and began conquering other civilizations. Spanish explorers who came to South America eventually conquered the Incas. Over the centuries many groups moved to South America, including Asians and Africans.		

DETAILS	KNOWLEDGE	INFERENCE
	Few people live in mountainous and desert areas. Rivers are important for agriculture and transportation. Natural resources are valuable. People usually live in places where the temperatures are mild and cool.	

Use after reading Chapter 7, pages 218–245.

© Harcourt

Name _____ Date _____

7 Test Preparation

Directions Read each question and choose the best answer. Then fill in the circle for the answer you have chosen. Be sure to fill in the circle completely.

1 The _____ is one of the driest places on Earth.
- Ⓐ Gran Chaco
- Ⓑ Atacama Desert
- Ⓒ Patagonia
- Ⓓ Tierra del Fuego

2 The Amazon River is very important to trade in the area because—
- Ⓕ it carries one-fifth of Earth's fresh river water.
- Ⓖ it is a source of water for irrigation.
- Ⓗ it contains the largest amount of freshwater fish.
- Ⓙ it provides a transportation corridor.

3 Which group developed the first known civilization in South America?
- Ⓐ Incas
- Ⓑ Chavins
- Ⓒ Ges
- Ⓓ Mochicas

4 What percent of South America's population lives in urban areas?
- Ⓕ 70%
- Ⓖ 49%
- Ⓗ 80%
- Ⓙ 65%

5 A South American country that won its independence peacefully is—
- Ⓐ Bolivia.
- Ⓑ Peru.
- Ⓒ Brazil.
- Ⓓ Argentina.

© Harcourt

Use after reading Chapter 7, pages 218–245.

Islands, Peninsulas, and Mountains

Directions Study the map below. Then use the map to help you answer the questions about Europe on page 72.

Europe

ICELAND

0 150 300 Miles
0 150 300 Kilometers
Azimuthal Equal-Area Projection

ATLANTIC OCEAN

SCANDINAVIAN PENINSULA

FINLAND

NORWAY

SWEDEN

ESTONIA

RUSSIA

LATVIA

LITHUANIA

RUSSIA

BELARUS

UNITED KINGDOM

JUTLAND

DENMARK

PENINSULA

IRELAND

Mountains of Kerry

Thames River

English Channel

NETH.

GREAT EUROPEAN PLAIN

GERMANY

Rhine R.

POLAND

UKRAINE

BELGIUM

LUXEMBOURG

LIECH.

Danube

CZECH REPUBLIC

SLOVAKIA

MOLDOVA

FRANCE

CENTRAL UPLANDS

SWITZ.

ALPS

AUSTRIA

SLOV.

HUNGARY

ROMANIA

R.

Danube R.

PYRENEES

APENNINES

CROATIA

BOS.-HERZ.

SERBIA

BALKANS

BULGARIA

PORTUGAL

ANDORRA

APENNINE PENINSULA

ITALY

MONTENEGRO

MAC.

ALBANIA

TURKEY

SPAIN

IBERIAN PENINSULA

SIERRA NEVADA

GREECE

BALKAN PENINSULA

Mediterranean

Sea

(continued)

© Harcourt

Name _____ Date _____

1 Which three countries in Western Europe have more than one mountain range located in them? _____

2 Which Western European peninsula that lies to the north has only one country located on it? _____

3 Which Western European country is made up of more than one island?

_____

4 Which two Western European countries have coasts on both the Mediterranean Sea and the Atlantic Ocean? _____

5 In which two Western European countries can you find parts of the Alps and the Great European Plain? _____

6 Which Western European countries are on the Iberian Peninsula?

_____

7 Which Western European country is on the Balkan Peninsula?

_____

8 Which river passes through the most Western European countries?

_____

9 In which Western European country are the Sierra Nevada Mountains?

_____

10 What is the name of the body of water that separates the United Kingdom from the European mainland? _____

© Harcourt

Use after reading Chapter 8, Lesson 1, pages 260–265.

Name _____ Date _____

MAP AND GLOBE SKILLS
Land Use and Products

Directions Study the products map of Germany below. Then answer the
questions on page 74.

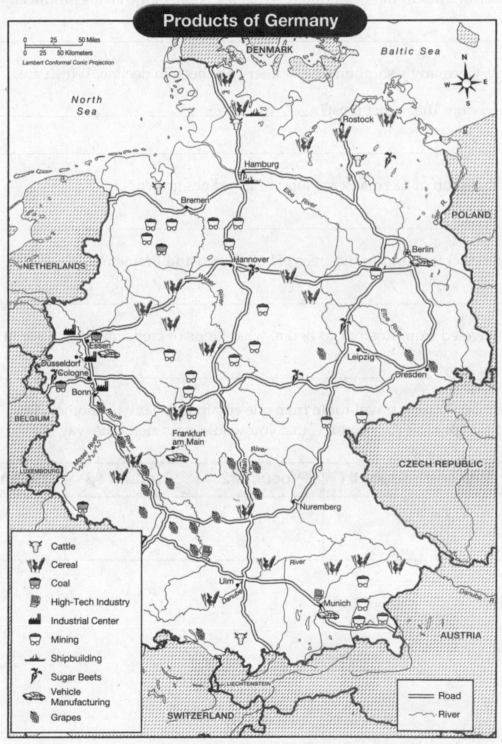

Products of Germany

0   25   50 Miles
0   25   50 Kilometers
Lambert Conformal Conic Projection

DENMARK   Baltic Sea

North
Sea   Rostock

Hamburg

Bremen   Elbe River   POLAND

Oder R.

NETHERLANDS   Hannover   Berlin

Weser River   Elbe River

Essen   Leipzig
Düsseldorf   Dresden
Cologne

Bonn
Rhine
BELGIUM   River   Frankfurt
am Main   River
LUXEMBOURG   Main River   CZECH REPUBLIC
Mosel River

Nuremberg

River

Ulm   Danube   Danube R.
Munich

AUSTRIA

LIECHTENSTEIN

SWITZERLAND

Legend

	Cattle
	Cereal
	Coal
	High-Tech Industry
	Industrial Center
	Mining
	Shipbuilding
	Sugar Beets
	Vehicle Manufacturing
	Grapes

Road
River

(continued)

© Harcourt

Name _____ Date _____

Directions Use the map on page 73 to answer the questions below.

1 Which area of Germany has the most manufacturing and industry?

_____

2 Circle Berlin, the capital of Germany. What are some of the area's products?

_____

3 Recently, Germany's shipbuilding industry has been in decline. Which area of

Germany does this affect most? _____

_____

4 In which region of Germany are most of its grapes grown?

_____

5 What product is found in the areas of both Essen and Bremen?

_____

6 If you traveled from Rostock to Berlin, what kinds of crops might you see in fields

along the way? _____

7 On the map, draw a travel route from one city in Germany to another. Then list
three different kinds of products that you would pass along the way.

Starting City	Product #1	Product #2	Product #3	Ending City

Use after reading Chapter 8, Skill Lesson, pages 266–267.

© Harcourt

Western Europe Through the Ages

Directions Match the events from Western European history listed in Box A with the effects that they helped cause listed in Box B. Write the letter of each effect in the space provided. Use your textbook to help you complete the activity.

Box A

Cause

_____ **1** Alexander the Great builds a huge empire.

_____ **2** The Roman Empire conquers much of Europe.

_____ **3** The Roman Empire falls.

_____ **4** Johannes Gutenberg invents a new way to print books.

_____ **5** Mercantilism becomes the new economic system.

_____ **6** Advances in science introduce new ways of manufacturing.

_____ **7** Countries compete for wealth and colonies.

_____ **8** World War I destroys much of Western Europe.

Box B

Effect

a. People develop strong feelings of nationalism.

b. Latin becomes the basis for many languages now spoken in Europe.

c. Information begins to spread more quickly.

d. Dictators come to power in several European nations.

e. People begin to move from farms to cities.

f. Western European nations set up colonies around the world.

g. Greek culture is spread.

h. Art, education, industry, and trade are nearly forgotten.

Directions Review the events above. Then choose one event and explain the cause and its effect in detail.

_____

_____

_____

_____

_____

Culture Unites and Culture Divides

Directions Read the passages below about Western European culture. Then read the statements that follow them. Decide whether each statement is a fact or an opinion, and explain your choice.

1 Many languages are spoken in Western Europe. Some countries, such as Switzerland, have several official languages. Others, such as France, have only one. In the United Kingdom, people speak English, but with different accents. Many people in Western Europe also speak some English.

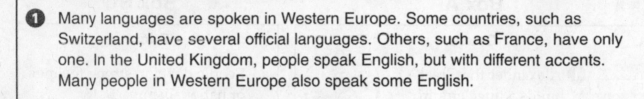

FACT or OPINION: English is the best language for people to speak.

_____

_____

2 Although most people in Western Europe are Roman Catholic, other religions are also practiced in the region. Some people practice Protestantism, a group of Christian denominations that split away from the Roman Catholic Church 500 years ago. Protestants and Catholics fought long wars against each other. Although people are tolerant of different religions in most parts of Western Europe, there is still some conflict. Today Catholics and Protestants continue to fight in Northern Ireland.

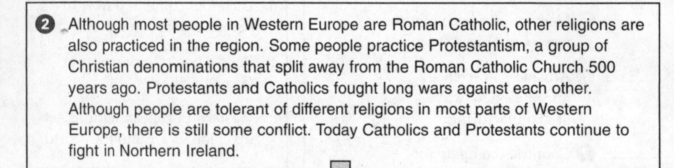

FACT or OPINION: Religious differences can lead to violence.

_____

_____

3 For hundreds of years, people have moved to Western Europe's cities in search of work. In the last century, many people have arrived from places such as Africa, Asia, Australia, and the Caribbean. In some countries migration has resulted in conflict. In other places, people from different ethnic groups have gotten along peacefully.

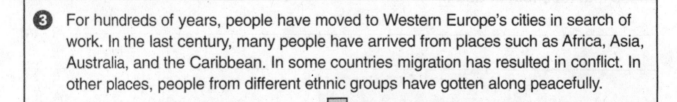

FACT or OPINION: Western Europe is very diverse culturally.

_____

Use after reading Chapter 8, Lesson 3, pages 276–281.

Name _____   Date _____

Unity in Europe

Directions The European Union is an important economic unit. It was originally formed in the 1950s as the European Coal and Steel Community and later became known as the European Community. Fill in the names of the countries that joined each form of the organization. Then read the statements that follow. Write the name of the country described by each statement. You may want to use your textbook or the Internet to help you complete the activity.

European Community
_____
_____
_____
_____
_____

European Economic Community
_____
_____
_____
_____
_____

European Union

Austria	Hungary	Poland
Cyprus	Latvia	Slovakia
Czech Republic	Lithuania	Slovenia
Estonia	Malta	Sweden
Finland		

1 This large republic, home to the *Train Grande Vitesse*, was one of the original members of the European Union. _____

2 This country is not a member of the European Union, although EU members surround it. _____

3 This northern country is famous for its shipyards.

_____

4 This tiny country was one of the original countries in the European Union. It is also famous for banking and finance. _____

5 This island country, which joined the European Community, was the first in which the rights of its citizens were protected. _____

© Harcourt

Name _____   Date _____

READING SKILLS
Read an Editorial Cartoon

Directions Examine the editorial cartoon below. Then answer the questions that follow it.

1 According to the sign, what does the mountain symbolize?

_____

2 What is the occupation of the two people on the mountain? Explain your answer.

_____

_____

3 What is the topic of this editorial cartoon? _____

_____

4 What do the two people think about the economy? _____

_____

5 What do you think the cartoonist thinks about this topic?

_____

Use after reading Chapter 8, Skill Lesson, pages 288-289.

Western Europe

Directions Complete this graphic organizer to show that you understand cause-and-effect relationships in Western Europe.

CAUSE		EFFECT

_____ → Much of northwestern Europe has a mild climate.

Gutenberg invented movable type. → _____

_____ → Europeans and Muslims began to exchange knowledge and ideas.

Religious and political differences exist between Catholics and Protestants in Northern Ireland. → _____

_____ → Many Western European nations have strong economies.

Name _____ Date _____

8 Test Preparation

Directions Read each question and choose the best answer. Then fill in the circle for the answer you have chosen. Be sure to fill in the circle completely.

1 Which of the following is NOT a major land region in the mainland of Western Europe?
Ⓐ the Great European Plain
Ⓑ the Central Uplands
Ⓒ the Alpine Mountain System
Ⓓ the Ruhr Valley

2 _____ was an economic system in which a nation's exports had to be greater than its imports.
Ⓕ Manorialism
Ⓖ Mercantilism
Ⓗ Socialism
Ⓙ Industrialism

3 The Western European country with three official languages is—
Ⓐ Spain.
Ⓑ Norway.
Ⓒ Switzerland.
Ⓓ Germany.

4 Many cities in Western Europe have been influenced by other cultures. In Cordoba, Spain, the _____ shows the influence of the Muslims who ruled parts of Spain.
Ⓕ food
Ⓖ theater
Ⓗ architecture
Ⓙ music

5 A major industry in France is—
Ⓐ agriculture.
Ⓑ natural gas.
Ⓒ coal.
Ⓓ iron ore.

Use after reading Chapter 8, pages 258–291.

Varied Lands and Varied Resources

Directions Study the chart below. It shows some of the countries of Eastern Europe, their special physical features, and their products. Use the chart to answer the questions on page 82.

Country	Physical Features	Products	
Czech Republic	Bohemian Forest Sudety Mountains	cement iron machinery plastic	pottery steel textiles wood
Estonia	low coastal plain thick forest 1,400 lakes 800 islands	farm products fish forest products oil shale	
Hungary	Danube River Tisza River thermal springs many lakes	fruits peppers vegetables	
Lithuania	low coastal plain thick forest	amber farm products fish forest products	
Macedonia	Balkan Mountains	cotton fruit rice	
Moldova	Dniester River Pruth River	tractors clothing corn	various consumer goods grapes
Poland	Vistula River Carpathian Mountains	automobiles machinery steel	
Romania	Carpathian Mountains Transylvanian Alps Danube River	farm products gold lignite silver	
Slovenia	Limestone caverns	forest products variety of crops	

© Harcourt

(continued)

Name _____ Date _____

1 How are the products of Lithuania and Estonia different?

_____

2 What physical feature do Poland and Romania have in common?

_____

3 Which country on the chart has the widest variety of products?

_____

4 Which two countries on the chart do not have products grown on farms?

_____

5 Which two countries on the chart rely on farming for all their major products?

_____

Directions Use the chart and your textbook to write a descriptive paragraph that compares two countries of Eastern Europe. Be sure to include the countries' physical features and products.

_____

_____

_____

_____

_____

_____

_____

_____

_____

_____

_____

© Harcourt

Centuries of Change

Directions The Eastern European countries were invaded many times and were ruled by many different conquerors. Using the information in your textbook, write the names of the invaders and rulers from the list below next to their descriptions in the chart. Some names may be used more than once, and others may not be used at all.

Invaders and Rulers

Huns	Poland
Russia	Austria-Hungary
Magyars	Byzantine Empire
Ottoman Empire	Soviet Union
Visigoths	Slavs

1	These people moved through the Carpathian Mountains and settled in what is now Hungary.	
2	This empire controlled the southern region of Eastern Europe by 1680.	
3	This country divided up Poland with Austria and Prussia, taking all the eastern areas of Poland.	
4	This country took control of Bosnia and Herzegovina in 1908.	
5	This empire lost Hungary to Austria in the 1700s.	
6	This country set up communist-style governments in many countries after World War II.	
7	This country was divided up into many smaller countries after World War I.	
8	This migrating people from Asia traveled to Eastern Europe.	
9	This empire lasted almost 1,000 years after splitting from the Western Roman Empire.	
10	These people settled what is now Poland, the Czech Republic, Slovakia, and the western Balkan countries.	

Name _____ Date _____

MAP AND GLOBE SKILLS
Identify Changing Borders

Poland Before Partition (1763)

RUSSIAN EMPIRE
Baltic Sea
Riga
PRUSSIA
Danzig
Vilna
Minsk
Posen
POLAND
Warsaw
Kiev
N
Cracow
Lemberg
W E
S
AUSTRIA

Legend:
Poland
Russia
Ottoman Empire
Prussia
Austria

Poland After First Partition (1772)

Riga
Baltic Sea
Danzig
Vilna
PRUSSIA
Minsk
RUSSIAN EMPIRE
Posen
POLAND
Warsaw
Kiev
Cracow
Lemberg
N
AUSTRIA
W E
S
OTTOMAN EMPIRE
Black Sea

Poland After Second Partition (1793)

Riga
Baltic Sea
Danzig
Vilna
Minsk
PRUSSIA
RUSSIAN EMPIRE
Posen
POLAND
Warsaw
Kiev
Cracow
Lemberg
N
AUSTRIA
W E
S
OTTOMAN EMPIRE
Black Sea

Poland After Third Partition (1795)

Riga
Baltic Sea
Danzig
Vilna
Minsk
PRUSSIA
RUSSIAN EMPIRE
Posen
Warsaw
Kiev
Cracow
Lemberg
N
AUSTRIA
W E
S
OTTOMAN EMPIRE
Black Sea

(continued)

Use after reading Chapter 9, Skill Lesson, pages 306–307.

Name _____ Date _____

Directions By comparing maps from different time periods, you can learn how the borders of countries have changed over time. Look at the maps on page 84 that show how Poland was divided at different times. Then answer the questions below.

1 Which countries increased their land area in 1772? _____

_____

2 Which country's borders did not change between 1793 and 1795?

_____

3 Which country lost territory in 1772, 1793, and 1795? _____

4 Which country added the largest amount of land to its territory between 1763 and 1795?

_____

5 Name the Polish cities that Prussia gained in 1772, 1793, and 1795.

_____

6 How did Prussia's borders change in 1772? _____

_____

7 Which countries did Russia border in 1772? _____

_____

8 The Polish cities listed below fell under foreign control during each of Poland's divisions. Sort the names of the cities by the year they fell under foreign control. Write each city's name in the correct column.

Danzig	Lemberg	Cracow	Minsk	Warsaw

1772	1793	1795
_____	_____	_____
_____	_____	_____

Times of Freedom

Directions Eastern Europe has undergone many changes since the fall of communism. Use the graphic organizer below to describe Eastern Europe after communist rule. Write three details to support each main idea.

Eastern Europe After Communism

The End of Communism

Trouble between ethnic groups has been a problem in Yugoslavia since the fall of communism.

_____

_____

_____

_____

_____

Forming New Governments

Many nations in Eastern Europe chose to set up democratic governments, but they had different forms.

_____

_____

_____

_____

_____

Changing Economies

People in Eastern Europe faced many difficulties as the industries in their countries were privatized.

_____

_____

_____

_____

Use after reading Chapter 9, Lesson 3, pages 308–313.

Varied Cultures

Directions Read each of the clues below. Use the clues to complete the crossword puzzle.

Across

2 Traditional Slovenian _____ is both beautiful and useful.

4 The _____ is a musical instrument in Moldova.

8 At dinner in Poland, you might be served a _____.

9 _____ wrote *Night*, a book about his experiences during the Holocaust. (two words)

10 _____ glass, made in the Czech Republic, is some of the best in the world.

Down

1 The _____ are a people who do not have a country of their own.

3 A traditional stringed instrument of Latvia is the _____.

5 The Hungarian composer _____ wrote many famous pieces of classical music. (two words)

6 A traditional salad eaten in Bulgaria is _____.

7 Many Hungarians eat _____, a spicy stew with many ingredients.

Use after reading Chapter 9, Lesson 4, pages 314–319.

Name _____ Date _____

Directions Read the description of a fictional conflict below. Then number the steps to show the order in which the conflict could be resolved.

Residents of a small town called Presno and the builders of its new airport are in conflict. Trucks carrying building materials to the construction site are driving very fast down Presno's main street. The residents of Presno are worried that their children may be hurt or killed by one of the fast-moving trucks. However, the construction crews need to get supplies to the construction site as quickly as possible. If they do not, the airport will not be finished on time and will cost much more money to complete.

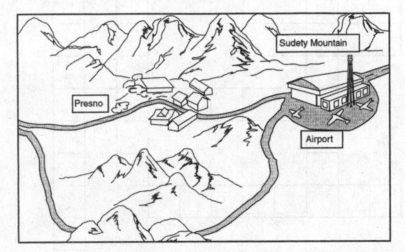

Step _____ The residents of Presno offer a compromise that during school hours, when children are indoors, the builders can send trucks through Presno to get to the airport more quickly. The remainder of the time, the trucks will go around Presno. The builders accept the compromise.

Step _____ The builders say that they will send their trucks through Presno more slowly but that they must use the most direct road possible. The residents say that is still too dangerous. They ask the builders to send some of their trucks around Presno.

Step _____ Both sides agree that they want the airport to be finished on time without anybody being hurt.

Step _____ Residents of Presno watch the trucks to make sure that they only drive through town during the scheduled hours. If they see a truck going through town when it should be driving around it, they report it to the builders and the police.

Step _____ The residents and the builders of the airport meet to discuss the issue. The residents ask the builders to send their trucks around Presno rather than through it. The builders believe that would take too long and slow down construction. Both groups go back and discuss what they can give up in order to reach an agreement.

Use after reading Chapter 9, Skill Lesson, pages 320–321.

Eastern Europe

Directions Complete this graphic organizer to show that you understand how to determine points of view about fighting in Kosovo.

SPEAKER	REASON FOR MAKING STATEMENT	POINT OF VIEW	WORDS THAT SIGNAL POINT OF VIEW
Bill Clinton, President of the United States	NATO's involvement in the bombings in Serbia		
Doug Hostetter, International Secretary of the Fellowship of Reconciliation	NATO's involvement in the bombings in Serbia		

Use after reading Chapter 9, pages 292–323.

Name _____   Date _____

9 Test Preparation

Directions Read each question and choose the best answer. Then fill in the circle for the answer you have chosen. Be sure to fill in the circle completely.

1 A natural feature that attracts visitors to the Czech Republic is the—
- Ⓐ Danube River.
- Ⓑ Carpathian Mountain Range.
- Ⓒ Thermal Spring.
- Ⓓ Bohemian Forest.

2 Which empire lasted almost 1,000 years by developing a strong government and economy?
- Ⓕ Ottoman
- Ⓖ Byzantine
- Ⓗ Roman
- Ⓙ Austrian

3 What happened at the end of World War I?
- Ⓐ The Ottoman Empire was created.
- Ⓑ New countries were formed in Eastern Europe.
- Ⓒ Austria-Hungary was united into one country.
- Ⓓ The Central Powers gained control of most of Eastern Europe.

4 Once new democracies were in place, the new privatized industries—
- Ⓕ were run by the governments.
- Ⓖ caused unemployment and inflation.
- Ⓗ flourished without government control.
- Ⓙ did not allow outside countries to bring in new business.

5 Paczki, shopska, and pierogi are all kinds of—
- Ⓐ traditional food.
- Ⓑ opera.
- Ⓒ rugs.
- Ⓓ stringed instruments.

© Harcourt

Use after reading Chapter 9, pages 292–323.

Landforms and Climates

Directions Use the map and clues below to help you unscramble the names of the countries and landforms in the Commonwealth of Independent States. Write the unscrambled words in the space provided.

1 the site of the Chernobyl disaster of 1986

_____
EANKURI

2 the "land of fire," where oil and natural gas are located

_____
ENIBZAAJRA

3 the barrier between Europe and Asia

_____
LAUR SNUTONMIA

4 the largest country in the world, stretching through Europe and Asia

_____
SIRASU

5 the country located in the Caucasus Mountains that has inactive volcanoes

_____
RANAIME

6 a country with many forests and rivers that provide its electricity

_____
USLAREB

7 the divider between the Caucasus Mountains and the desert countries

_____
IPNACSA EAS

© Harcourt

CHART AND GRAPH SKILLS
Read a Climograph

Directions Using the information in the tables below, complete the climographs for the capitals of Ukraine and Azerbaijan. You may want to use your textbook to help you complete the activity. Then answer the questions on page 93.

Kiev, Ukraine												
	JAN	FEB	MAR	APR	MAY	JUNE	JULY	AUG	SEP	OCT	NOV	DEC
Temperature (°F)	22°	24°	33°	48°	59°	65°	67°	66°	57°	47°	36°	28°
Precipitation (in.)	1.90	1.80	1.50	1.90	2.10	2.90	3.50	2.70	1.90	1.40	2.00	2.10

Baku, Azerbaijan												
	JAN	FEB	MAR	APR	MAY	JUNE	JULY	AUG	SEP	OCT	NOV	DEC
Temperature (°F)	38°	38°	42°	53°	62°	69°	75°	75°	68°	58°	50°	42°
Precipitation (in.)	0.90	0.90	1.00	0.70	0.60	0.20	0.10	0.30	0.70	1.10	1.40	1.10

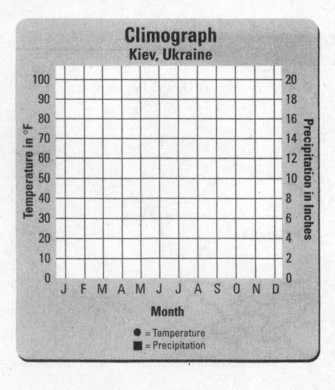

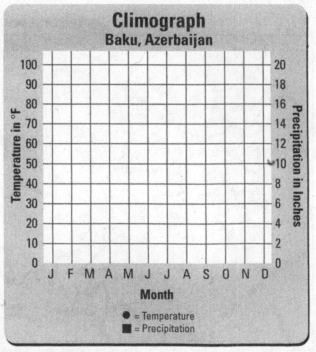

(continued)

Use after reading Chapter 10, Skill Lesson, pages 332–333.

Name _____ Date _____

1 Which city has a winter with more precipitation? _____

2 Which city has a warmer winter? _____

3 During which months is Baku the hottest? _____

4 During which season does Baku get the most rain? During which season does it get

the least rain? _____

5 Cotton grows best in warmer areas where the temperature does not usually drop
below freezing. If you were going to plant cotton near one of these cities, which of

the two cities would you choose? Explain your answer. _____

_____

_____

6 Corn grows best in areas that receive 18 to 25 inches of rain a year. If you were going
to plant corn near one of these cities, which of the two cities would you choose?

Explain your answer. _____

_____

_____

7 If farmers usually plant corn when the temperature of the soil reaches 55°
Fahrenheit, during which month might you plant corn near the city you chose in

number six? Explain your answer. _____

_____

© Harcourt

Name _____ Date _____

The Soviet Union Rises and Falls

Directions Study the time line of Russian history. Use the time line to answer the questions.

1880

1890
• 1894
Nicholas II comes to power

• 1905
Bloody Sunday

1900
• 1917
Russian Revolution begins,
and Nicholas II abdicates

1910

• 1918
Nicholas II is executed

1920
• 1922
Lenin and Bolsheviks form
the Soviet Union

1930
• 1924
Stalin becomes leader of
Soviet Union

1940

• 1945
USSR begins taking control
of Central and Eastern Europe

1950

1960

1970

• 1985
Mikhail Gorbachev becomes
leader of USSR

1980

• 1991
Gorbachev steps down, and
the Soviet Union comes to an end

1990

2000
• 2000
Vladimir Putin is elected as
new leader of Russia

1 How long after the Russian Revolution began did Lenin and the Bolsheviks form the Soviet Union? _____

2 Who was the last czar of Russia?

_____

3 How long did the Soviet Union last?

_____

4 How long was Mikhail Gorbachev the leader of the Soviet Union? _____

5 Who was elected the leader of Russia in 2000?

_____

Directions Write a paragraph describing the events of the Russian Revolution and the founding of the Soviet Union. Use the information in the time line and your textbook.

_____

_____

_____

_____

_____

© Harcourt

Use after reading Chapter 10, Lesson 2, pages 334–339.

MAP AND GLOBE SKILLS
Read a Time Zone Map

Directions The Commonwealth of Independent States includes many different time zones. Study the time zone map below. Then complete the activities on page 96.

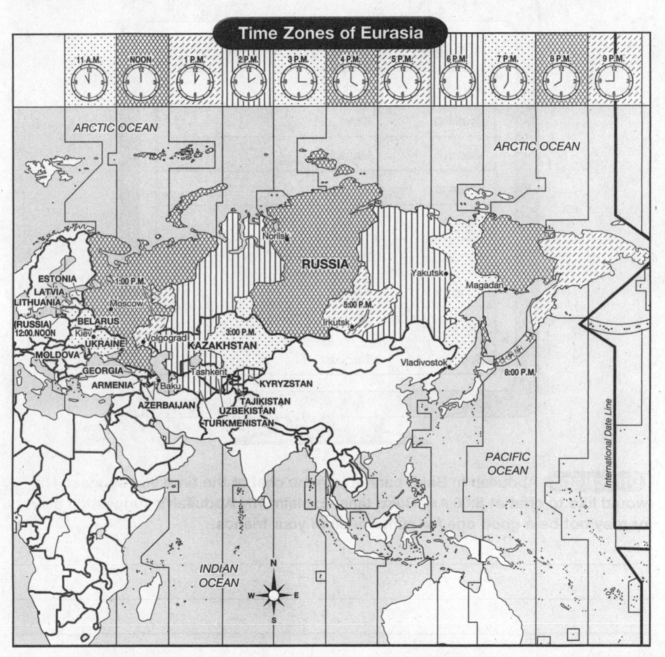

(continued)

© Harcourt

Name _____ Date _____

Directions Imagine that you live in Moscow and want to schedule an online chat with your friends in cities across the CIS. The time differences between the cities make communicating with your friends difficult. Use the time zone map on page 95 to help you fill in the local time each of your friends would need to join a chat with you at noon Moscow time.

Friend	City	Time
Anya	Norilsk	
Svetlana	Kiev	
Vladimir	Magadan	
Katerina	Volgograd	
Mikhail	Irkutsk	
Abdullah	Baku	
Natasha	Yakutsk	
Raisa	Vladivostok	
Sophia	Tashkent	

Directions Abdullah in Baku cannot join the chat at the time you suggest. He would like to chat at 8:00 P.M. Baku time. Explain why Abdullah's suggestion may or may not be a good one for some or all of your friends.

_____

_____

_____

      Use after reading Chapter 10, Skill Lesson, pages 340–341.

Times of Change

Directions Many aspects of life in the Commonwealth of Independent States (CIS) have changed since the fall of the Soviet Union. Use the information in your textbook to complete the tables below. In some places you will have to write about what life was like under the Soviet Union. In other places you will have to write about what life was like after the Soviet Union.

Under the Soviet Union . . .	After the Soviet Union . . .
❶ Large sports arenas were built.	Most large sports arenas are closed.
❷ _____	People begin to practice religion openly.
❸ _____	Many businesses are sold to private owners and private companies.
❹ People were guaranteed jobs, but they could not choose the jobs they wanted.	_____
❺ The space program was failing because there was not enough money.	_____
❻ There were no wealthy social classes.	_____

Directions Choose another aspect of life in the CIS, such as culture, language, food, athletics, or city life. Explain how that aspect of life has or has not changed since the fall of the Soviet Union.

_____

_____

_____

_____

Use after reading Chapter 10, Lesson 3, pages 342–347.

Name _____ Date _____

Russia and the Eurasian Republics

Directions Complete this graphic organizer to show that you understand how to categorize different landforms in Russia.

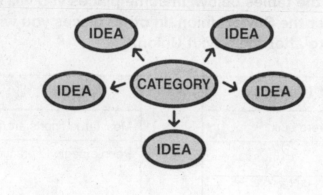

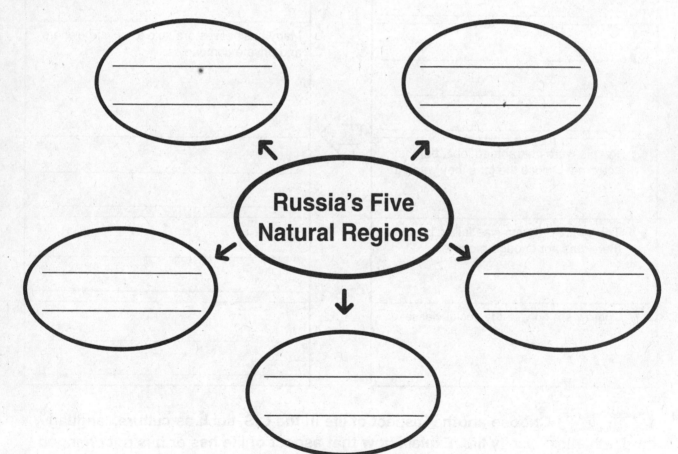

Russia's Five Natural Regions

Use after reading Chapter 10, pages 324–349.

© Harcourt

Name _____ Date _____

10 Test Preparation

Directions Read each question and choose the best answer. Then fill in the circle for the answer you have chosen. Be sure to fill in the circle completely.

1 What forms a natural barrier between Europe and Asia?
- Ⓐ the Volga River
- Ⓑ the Ural Mountains
- Ⓒ the Siberian Lowlands
- Ⓓ the Northern European Plains

2 _____ covers 233,000 square miles and is about the size of Texas.
- Ⓕ Kazakhstan
- Ⓖ Belarus
- Ⓗ Russia
- Ⓙ Ukraine

3 What brought an end to the rule of the czars in Russia?
- Ⓐ the Russian Revolution and the establishment of communism
- Ⓑ the death of Catherine the Great
- Ⓒ the rule of the dictator Stalin
- Ⓓ World War II

4 Boris Yeltsin became Russia's first democratic leader in—
- Ⓕ 1985.
- Ⓖ 1989.
- Ⓗ 1993.
- Ⓙ 1991.

5 Before the fall of the Soviet Union, citizens in the Commonwealth of Independent States were not allowed to—
- Ⓐ play chess.
- Ⓑ tell folktales.
- Ⓒ practice religion.
- Ⓓ eat traditional foods.

© Harcourt

Use after reading Chapter 10, pages 324–349.

Name _____ Date _____

Land of Contrasts

Directions Study the map of Southwest Asia. Then read the sentences that follow. Provide supporting details for each sentence, using information from the map and your textbook. Use a separate sheet of paper, if necessary.

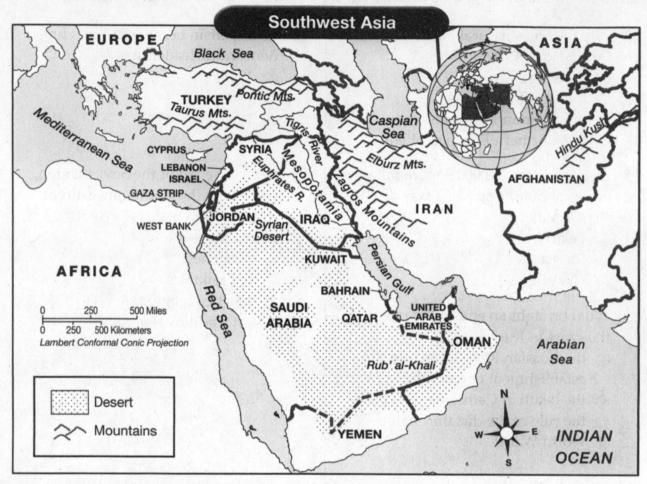

① Southwest Asia has many different physical features and is more than a region

of deserts. _____

_____

_____

② Southwest Asia has many natural resources other than oil.

_____

_____

_____

Use after reading Chapter 11, Lesson 1, pages 364–370.

SOCIAL STUDIES

Can also be used with
Houghton Mifflin Social Studies

Homework and Practice Books
and **Activity Books** provide study
guides and activities to support

Reading Support and
Intervention and Reading
Support and Test Prep offer
various lesson-by-lesson support
for improving text comprehension,
vocabulary/concept words, and
building fluency.

Reading Support and Intervention

Grade 1	978-0-15-349427-7	$60.70
Grade 2	978-0-15-349428-4	60.70
Grade 3	978-0-15-349429-1	60.70

Assessment Programs contain
copying masters of chapter,
summative, and unit tests, as
well as individual and group
performance assessments.

Grade 1	978-0-15-347306-7	$48.90
Grade 2	978-0-15-347307-4	48.90
Grade 3	978-0-15-347308-1	64.85
States and Regions	978-0-15-347309-8	93.80
The United States	978-0-15-347310-4	120.85
The United States: Making a New Nation	978-0-15-347311-1	120.85
The United States: Civil War to Present	978-0-15-347312-8	120.85
Ancient Civilizations	978-0-15-347313-5	120.85
World History	978-0-15-354251-0	120.85
World Regions	978-0-15-356689-9	123.25

content and skills taught in the Student Editions.

Homework and Practice Books

Grade 1	978-0-15-347292-3	$6.85
Grade 2	978-0-15-347293-0	7.90
Grade 3	978-0-15-347294-7	7.90
States and Regions	978-0-15-347295-4	8.70
The United States	978-0-15-347296-1	8.70
The United States: Making a New Nation	978-0-15-347297-8	8.70
The United States: Civil War to Present	978-0-15-347298-5	8.70
Ancient Civilizations	978-0-15-347299-2	8.70

Homework and Practice Book Teacher Editions

Homework and Practice Book Teacher Editions for grades K–2 are included in the grade-level Teacher Editions.

Grade 3	978-0-15-347300-5	19.55
States and Regions	978-0-15-347301-2	19.85
The United States: Making a New Nation	978-0-15-347302-9	21.05
The United States	978-0-15-347303-6	21.05
The United States: Civil War to Present	978-0-15-347304-3	21.05
Ancient Civilizations	978-0-15-347305-0	21.25

Activity Books

World History	978-0-15-354245-9	8.70
World Regions	978-0-15-356687-5	8.70

Activity Book Teacher Editions

World History	978-0-15-354248-0	21.25
World Regions	978-0-15-356688-2	21.70

0 102658643

V21818103

States and Regions	978-0-15-349430-7	60.70
The United States	978-0-15-349432-1	64.35
The United States: Making a New Nation	978-0-15-349431-4	64.35
The United States: Civil War to Present	978-0-15-349435-2	64.35
Ancient Civilizations	978-0-15-349436-9	64.35

Reading Support and Test Prep

World History	978-0-15-354990-8	10.50
World History, Answer Key	978-0-15-354263-3	22.95

Success for English Language Learners builds proficiency in

listening/speaking, writing, and reading skills and aides in developing academic language, building background, scaffolding content, and applying and assessing student understanding.

Grade 1	978-0-15-349405-5	$60.70
Grade 2	978-0-15-349406-2	60.70
Grade 3	978-0-15-349407-9	60.70
States and Regions	978-0-15-349408-6	64.35
The United States	978-0-15-349414-7	64.35
The United States: Making a New Nation	978-0-15-349409-3	64.35
The United States: Civil War to Present	978-0-15-349415-4	64.35
Ancient Civilizations	978-0-15-349416-1	64.35

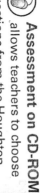

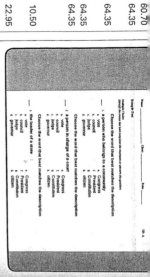

Assessment on CD-ROM

allows teachers to choose questions from the Houghton Mifflin Harcourt School Publishers item bank or create their own test questions, then print the test. Powered by ExamView®.

Grade 1	978-0-15-351977-2	$131.20
Grade 2	978-0-15-351978-9	131.20
Grade 3	978-0-15-351979-6	131.20
States and Regions	978-0-15-351980-2	131.20
The United States	978-0-15-351982-6	131.20
The United States: Making a New Nation	978-0-15-351981-9	131.20
The United States: Civil War to Present ..	978-0-15-351983-3	131.20
Ancient Civilizations	978-0-15-351984-0	131.20

For all system requirements, go to www.hmhschool.com/techsupport

2009 Pre-K–8

Southwest Asia Long Ago

Directions Read the statement about each historical event below. Use your textbook and other reference materials to help you find the year that each event occurred. Write the year of each event on the line provided.

_____ Sargon creates the Akkadian Empire by capturing all the Mesopotamian city-states.

_____ The land that was once the kingdom of Israel falls under Roman control.

_____ Sumerian communities grow into city-states.

_____ The Persian Empire reaches from Egypt to India.

_____ By this date, Hammurabi has conquered much of Mesopotamia, forming the Babylonian Empire.

_____ Alexander the Great conquers the Persian Empire.

Directions Study the dates on the time line below. Place each event above in its correct place on the time line.

Southwest Asia Long Ago

| 4000 B.C. | 3500 B.C. | 3000 B.C. | 2500 B.C. | 2000 B.C. | 1500 B.C. | 1000 B.C. | 500 B.C. | A.D. 1 |

_____

_____   _____   _____

_____   _____   _____

_____   _____   _____

_____   _____   _____

_____   _____

_____

© Harcourt

Name _____ Date _____

Compare Historical Maps

Directions Study the maps below. Pay close attention to the information that they provide about Southwest Asia at different time periods. Use the maps to help you complete the activities that follow.

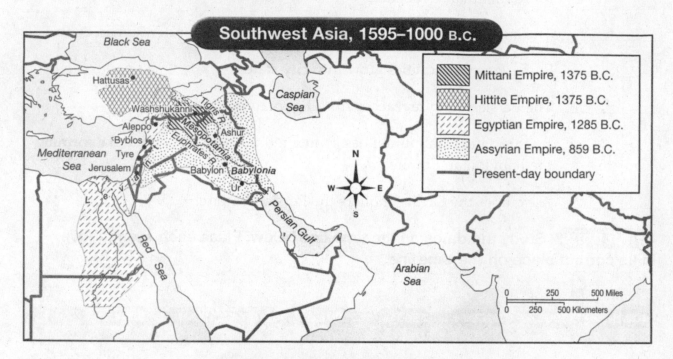

Southwest Asia, 1595–1000 B.C.

Mittani Empire, 1375 B.C.
Hittite Empire, 1375 B.C.
Egyptian Empire, 1285 B.C.
Assyrian Empire, 859 B.C.
Present-day boundary

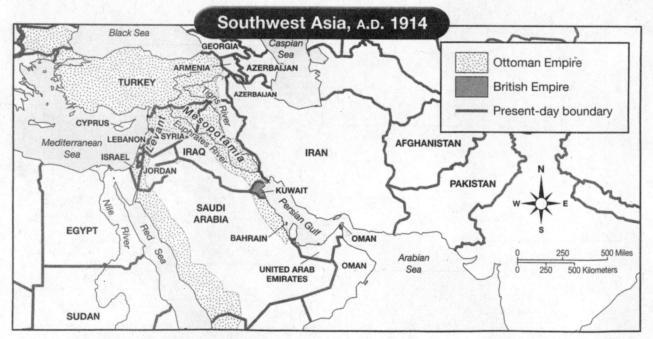

Southwest Asia, A.D. 1914

Ottoman Empire
British Empire
Present-day boundary

(continued)

Use after reading Chapter 11, Skill Lesson, pages 378–379.

Name _____ Date _____

Directions Study the empires shown on page 102. Then find the names of countries that today occupy the land that belonged to these empires. Write the names of these countries on the lines below the empires.

1 Ottoman Empire

_____

_____

2 Assyrian Empire

_____

3 Mittani Empire

_____

4 Hittite Empire

_____

5 Egyptian Empire

_____

Directions Study the maps on page 102 to answer the following questions.

6 Write the names of the empires that conquered Mesopotamia in historical order.

_____

_____

7 Which empire on the maps was the last to control the country of Jordan?

_____

© Harcourt

Use after reading Chapter 11, Skill Lesson, pages 378–379.

Name _____   Date _____

Influences on Cultures

Directions Read the following paragraph. Use the information in the paragraph and your textbook to complete the chart below.

Many different groups of people live in Southwest Asia. The majority of these people are Arabs. They live in several of the countries in the region. Other groups, including Afghans, Greeks, Jews, and Iranians, live in different parts of Southwest Asia. Many of the Arab and Iranian peoples are Muslims. They belong to either the Sunni or Shi'i branches of Islam. Other groups, such as the Greek people of Cyprus, are Christians. The majority of the people of Israel are Jewish. Israel is the only country in the region where Judaism is the official religion.

Countries of Southwest Asia			
Country	**Ethnic Group(s)**	**Religious Practice(s)**	**Major Language(s)**
Afghanistan	Afghans	Sunni Muslim, Shi'i Muslim	
Bahrain			
Cyprus			
Iran			Farsi
Iraq			
Israel	Jews, Palestinians		Hebrew
Jordan			
Kuwait			
Lebanon	Arabs	many Muslim and Christian sects	Arabic
Oman			
Qatar			
Saudi Arabia			
Syria			
Turkey			
United Arab Emirates			
Yemen		Sunni Muslim, Shi'i Muslim	

© Harcourt

Use after reading Chapter 11, Lesson 3, pages 380–385.

New Governments and Strong Economies

Directions In each statement, underline the name of the correct country. Use the chart showing oil production in Southwest Asia to choose the countries being described.

1 (Kuwait/Saudi Arabia) produces just over 93 billion barrels of oil. It produces slightly more than the country of Iraq.

2 Oman produces slightly more oil than this country, but not much more. (Iran/Yemen) totals just over 3 billion barrels of oil each year.

3 (Iran/Kuwait)'s almost 90 billion barrels of oil each year make it Southwest Asia's fourth-largest oil producer.

4 (Bahrain/Syria) produces the least amount of oil in the entire region of Southwest Asia.

Oil Production in Southwest Asia

Countries	Oil Produced
Saudi Arabia	
Iraq	
Kuwait	
Iran	
United Arab Emirates	
Qatar	
Oman	
Yemen	
Syria	
Bahrain	

25 billion barrels of oil

10 billion barrels of oil

1 billion barrels of oil

Directions Read the question. Write your answer on the lines provided.

5 Several countries in Southwest Asia belong to the Organization of Petroleum Exporting Countries (OPEC). How does being a member of OPEC help the countries?

_____

_____

_____

_____

Name _____ Date _____

READING SKILLS
Identify Frames of Reference

Directions When learning about historical events, it is important to study different frames of reference and points of view. Read each point of view about a dam project on the Euphrates River. Then answer the questions that follow to help you understand the different frames of references.

"My family owned a wheat farm along the Euphrates River. Floods brought rich soil and water each year from the highlands. We always had plenty of water to irrigate our crop fields, and the harvests were very large. Then in the 1960s and 1970s, the people of Turkey began building dams that held back the water. The river no longer floods and there is little water. Today we can barely grow enough food to survive. I think the people of Turkey are stealing our water."

A Syrian farmer

"The people of Turkey have a right to use the natural resources within our borders. The dams offer the Turkish people water for their crops and an energy supply. Before these dams were built, the river's water levels were high. Some years there were damaging floods. Now our dams keep the flow of water even at all times. They also give the whole region a supply of hydroelectric power. The other countries should be grateful. When all of the dams are built, our neighbors will see how the dams benefit us all."

A Turkish government official

1 What is the problem? _____

_____

2 What does the Syrian farmer want? What does the Turkish government official want?

_____

_____

3 What is the Syrian farmer's frame of reference? How does it affect his point of view?

_____

_____

4 What is the Turkish official's frame of reference. How does it affect his point of view?

_____

_____

© Harcourt

Use after reading Chapter 11, Skill Lesson, pages 394–395.

Name _____ Date _____

MAP AND GLOBE SKILLS
Follow Routes on a Map

Directions Study the map of the ancient trade routes of Egypt. Pay close attention to both the land and the water routes. Then use the map to help you complete the activities that follow.

Ancient Egypt traded with several other civilizations around the known world. Egyptian merchants exchanged goods with the Libyan peoples to the west, African civilizations in the south, and the empires of Southwest Asia and Europe. Merchants traveled land and water routes that crossed the world to bring goods such as gold, turquoise, and wood to Egyptian temples and the pharaoh's court.

Trade Routes of Ancient Egypt

EUROPE
Black Sea
GREECE
Caspian Sea
pottery
ANATOLIA
HITTITE EMPIRE
CRETE
CYPRUS
copper
LEVANT
pottery
wood
Mediterranean Sea
ASIA
N
W E
S
CANAAN
pottery
livestock
copper
lead
granite
jasper
turquoise
Memphis
Sinai Peninsula
copper
LIBYA
EGYPTIAN EMPIRE
copper
limestone
Thebes
emeralds
gold
ARABIA
AFRICA
Nile River
gold
gold
NUBIA
gold
Red Sea
spices
ebony, ivory
Arabian Sea

0 250 500 Miles
0 250 500 Kilometers
Miller Cylindrical Projection

—— Land Route
---- Sea Route

© Harcourt

(continued)

Use after reading Chapter 12, Skill Lesson, pages 406–407.

Name _____ Date _____

Southwest Asia

Directions Complete this graphic organizer to show that you understand how to compare and contrast information about the influence of oil in Southwest Asia.

TOPIC A _____
TOPIC B _____

LIFE BEFORE THE DISCOVERY OF OIL	LIFE AFTER THE DISCOVERY OF OIL
_____ _____	Urban areas and cities began to grow.
People farmed and sold crops in markets.	_____
_____	Governments were able to pay for improved health care and education.
Food was sometimes in short supply.	_____

© Harcourt

Use after reading Chapter 11, pages 362–397.

Name _____ Date _____

11 Test Preparation

Directions Read each question and choose the best answer. Then fill in the circle for the answer you have chosen. Be sure to fill in the circle completely.

1 The Tigris and Euphrates Rivers come together in southeastern Iraq to form the—
Ⓐ Shatt al Arab.
Ⓑ Rub'al-Khali.
Ⓒ Jordan River.
Ⓓ Kuwait River.

2 Southwest Asia is a crossroads where Asia and Africa meet another continent. What is the name of the third continent?
Ⓕ North America
Ⓖ South America
Ⓗ Europe
Ⓙ Australia

3 An ancient Sumerian city-state—
Ⓐ had a group of leaders.
Ⓑ had a temple called a ziggurat.
Ⓒ had a religion based on worshiping one God.
Ⓓ had no form of writing or language for record keeping.

4 Islamic laws discourage images of people or animals. Which image might be found in a piece of Islamic art?
Ⓕ coins and sword dancers
Ⓖ people relaxing on a beach
Ⓗ horses and bulls
Ⓙ geometric shapes

5 At the end of World War I, the Allied Powers took most of the defeated Ottoman Empire's land. The land left in Ottoman control became which country?
Ⓐ Israel
Ⓑ Syria
Ⓒ Turkey
Ⓓ Saudi Arabia

© Harcourt

Use after reading Chapter 11, pages 362–397.

Name _____ Date _____

A Region of Deserts

Directions The geography of North Africa is harsh. Yet it is home to millions of people. Read each of the main ideas about the geography of North Africa. For each main idea, write three details that support it.

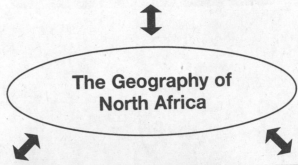

COASTAL PLAIN

The coastal plain is an ideal place for much of the region's population.

1 _____

2 _____

3 _____

The Geography of North Africa

NILE RIVER

The Nile River is an important resource for the people of Egypt.

1 _____

2 _____

3 _____

THE SAHARA

The Sahara is mostly barren, but has some resources for the region's people.

1 _____

2 _____

3 _____

© Harcourt

Use after reading Chapter 12, Lesson 1, pages 400–405.

Southwest Asia

Directions Complete this graphic organizer to show that you understand how to compare and contrast information about the influence of oil in Southwest Asia.

TOPIC A	TOPIC B
_____	_____
_____	_____

LIFE BEFORE THE DISCOVERY OF OIL

_____

_____

People farmed and sold crops in markets.

_____

_____

Food was sometimes in short supply.

LIFE AFTER THE DISCOVERY OF OIL

Urban areas and cities began to grow.

_____

_____

Governments were able to pay for improved health care and education.

_____

_____

Use after reading Chapter 11, pages 362–397.

Name _____   Date _____

11 Test Preparation

Directions Read each question and choose the best answer. Then fill in the circle for the answer you have chosen. Be sure to fill in the circle completely.

1 The Tigris and Euphrates Rivers come together in southeastern Iraq to form the—
Ⓐ Shatt al Arab.
Ⓑ Rub'al-Khali.
Ⓒ Jordan River.
Ⓓ Kuwait River.

2 Southwest Asia is a crossroads where Asia and Africa meet another continent. What is the name of the third continent?
Ⓕ North America
Ⓖ South America
Ⓗ Europe
Ⓙ Australia

3 An ancient Sumerian city-state—
Ⓐ had a group of leaders.
Ⓑ had a temple called a ziggurat.
Ⓒ had a religion based on worshiping one God.
Ⓓ had no form of writing or language for record keeping.

4 Islamic laws discourage images of people or animals. Which image might be found in a piece of Islamic art?
Ⓕ coins and sword dancers
Ⓖ people relaxing on a beach
Ⓗ horses and bulls
Ⓙ geometric shapes

5 At the end of World War I, the Allied Powers took most of the defeated Ottoman Empire's land. The land left in Ottoman control became which country?
Ⓐ Israel
Ⓑ Syria
Ⓒ Turkey
Ⓓ Saudi Arabia

Use after reading Chapter 11, pages 362–397.

© Harcourt

A Region of Deserts

Directions The geography of North Africa is harsh. Yet it is home to millions of people. Read each of the main ideas about the geography of North Africa. For each main idea, write three details that support it.

COASTAL PLAIN

The coastal plain is an ideal place for much of the region's population.

1 _____

2 _____

3 _____

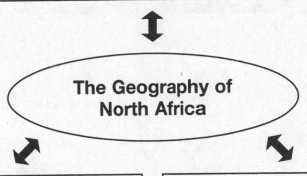

The Geography of North Africa

NILE RIVER

The Nile River is an important resource for the people of Egypt.

1 _____

_____

2 _____

_____

3 _____

_____

THE SAHARA

The Sahara is mostly barren, but has some resources for the region's people.

1 _____

_____

2 _____

_____

3 _____

_____

MAP AND GLOBE SKILLS

Follow Routes on a Map

Directions Study the map of the ancient trade routes of Egypt. Pay close attention to both the land and the water routes. Then use the map to help you complete the activities that follow.

Ancient Egypt traded with several other civilizations around the known world. Egyptian merchants exchanged goods with the Libyan peoples to the west, African civilizations in the south, and the empires of Southwest Asia and Europe. Merchants traveled land and water routes that crossed the world to bring goods such as gold, turquoise, and wood to Egyptian temples and the pharaoh's court.

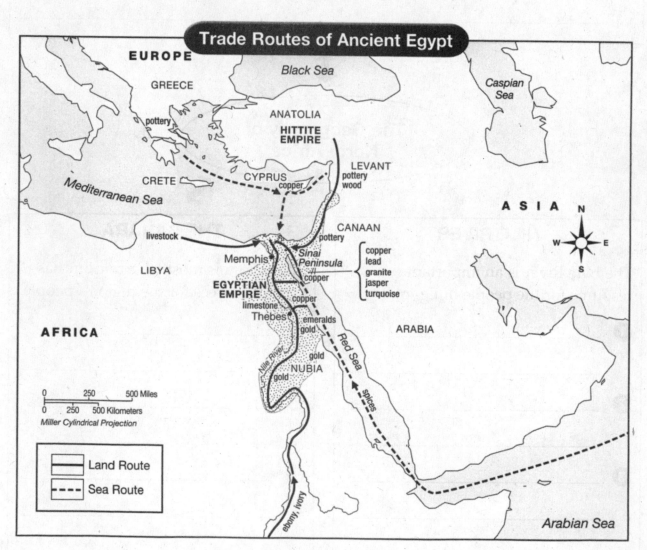

Trade Routes of Ancient Egypt

(continued)

Use after reading Chapter 12, Skill Lesson, pages 406–407.

Name _____ Date _____

Directions Imagine you are an ancient Egyptian merchant. The pharaoh needs several products for the royal temples and palaces at Thebes. Read the list below. Then plan a trade mission to find the goods, using the shortest route possible. Draw your route on the map, starting at Memphis. Then describe the route in the space below.

Wood for the river barges	Horses to pull the royal chariots
Copper for royal mirrors and tools	Turquoise for jewelry

_____

_____

_____

_____

Directions The pharaoh has demanded more goods. Study the map and answer the questions to meet his needs.

1 Where might you find ebony for the pharaoh? _____

_____

2 If you are in the city of Thebes, in which direction would you travel to find

the ebony? _____

3 In which direction from Thebes would you find emeralds? _____

4 If you were in the Nile Delta, how would you travel to find pottery for the

pharaoh's palaces? _____

_____

5 From the Nile Delta, where would you find the closest source of copper and

turquoise, and how might you get there? _____

_____

_____

© Harcourt

Name _____ Date _____

Ancient Days to Independence

Directions The natural resources in and around the Nile River had many effects on life in ancient Egypt. Read each pair of statements about the Egyptian civilization. Decide which is the cause and which is the effect. Write the letter C (Cause) or E (Effect) on the lines to identify the statements.

1 _____ The Nile River floods carried rich soils and inundated the land along the river bank.

_____ Egyptian farmers planted and harvested crops in the rich soil along the river bank.

2 _____ The Egyptians believed that they would live again after death.

_____ The Egyptians saw the sun rise and fall and thought it was a god who was born each morning and died each night.

3 _____ The Egyptian farmers worked on the pharaoh's building projects.

_____ The Nile River floods covered the crop fields for weeks, preventing any planting.

4 _____ Egypt became a wealthy nation because of its rich soil and many crops.

_____ Egypt's enemies wanted to conquer the kingdom to control its resources.

Directions Some effects become the causes of other effects. Study each picture and read its statement. Determine if it could be the cause of another effect. Then number each of the statements in the order that they might occur as a series of causes and effects.

_____  Tombs were built to house the objects a person would need in his or her afterlife.

_____  The Egyptians believed they would have an afterlife.

_____  The vegetation in the Nile Valley died after each harvest, and then the season changed.

_____  The Nile Valley came back to life after each inundation.

_____  The Egyptians developed ways of preserving dead bodies.

Use after reading Chapter 12, Lesson 2, pages 408–413.

© Harcourt

Name _____ Date _____

CHART AND GRAPH SKILLS
Read a Telescoping Time Line

Directions The time line below shows some of the key dates in the history of North Africa. One section of the time line has been expanded to help you take a closer look at events that happened in recent times. Use both parts of the time line to answer the questions on page 114.

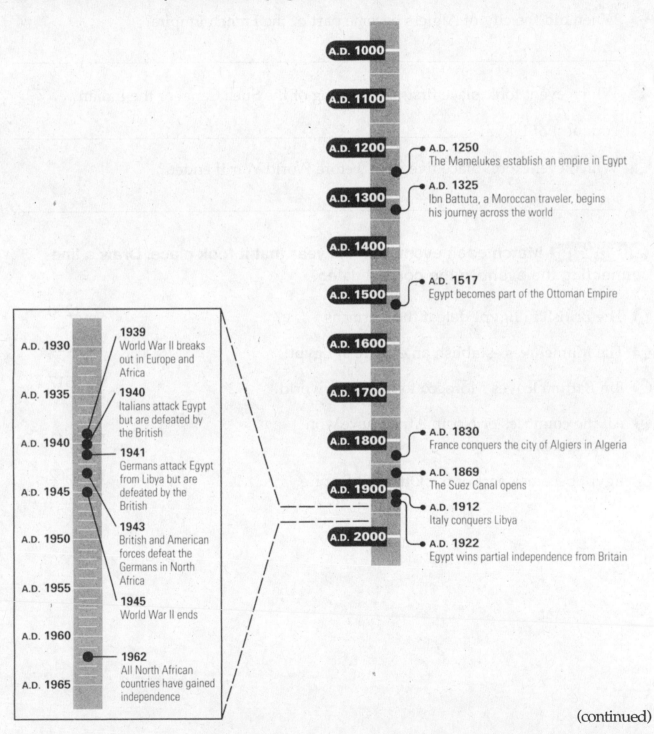

A.D. 1000

A.D. 1100

A.D. 1200

A.D. 1250
The Mamelukes establish an empire in Egypt

A.D. 1300

A.D. 1325
Ibn Battuta, a Moroccan traveler, begins his journey across the world

A.D. 1400

A.D. 1517
Egypt becomes part of the Ottoman Empire

A.D. 1500

A.D. 1600

A.D. 1700

A.D. 1830
France conquers the city of Algiers in Algeria

A.D. 1800

A.D. 1869
The Suez Canal opens

A.D. 1900

A.D. 1912
Italy conquers Libya

A.D. 2000

A.D. 1922
Egypt wins partial independence from Britain

A.D. 1930

1939
World War II breaks out in Europe and Africa

A.D. 1935

1940
Italians attack Egypt but are defeated by the British

A.D. 1940

1941
Germans attack Egypt from Libya but are defeated by the British

A.D. 1945

1943
British and American forces defeat the Germans in North Africa

A.D. 1950

1945
World War II ends

A.D. 1955

A.D. 1960

1962
All North African countries have gained independence

A.D. 1965

© Harcourt

(continued)

Name _____ Date _____

1 What time period does the time line show? What time period does the

telescoping part of the time line show? _____

_____

2 According to the time line, which group conquered Egypt first? How long did

they rule Egypt? _____

3 When did the city of Algiers become part of the French Empire?

_____

4 Which event took place first, the opening of the Suez Canal or the Italian

conquest of Libya? _____

5 Which event took place five years before World War II ended?

_____

Directions **Match each event with the year that it took place. Draw a line connecting the event to the correct date.**

6 The British in Egypt defeat the Germans.   **A.** 1250

7 The Mamelukes establish an empire in Egypt.   **B.** 1325

8 Ibn Battuta leaves Morocco to travel the world.   **C.** 1517

9 All the countries of North Africa have won
independence.   **D.** 1941

10 Egypt becomes part of the Ottoman Empire.   **E.** 1962

© Harcourt

Name _____   Date _____

A Blend of Cultures

Directions Anthropologists are people who study the societies and cultures of other peoples. Imagine that you are an anthropologist traveling in North Africa to study either a Berber or Bedouin group. Write a journal entry that describes what it is like to live with one of these groups. Make sure your journal answers the questions below.

❶ Where does your group live? Draw a map in the box to the right that shows its location.

❷ What languages do the people in your group speak?

❸ How is the group's way of life different from other ways of life in the region?

❹ How has your group resisted changes to the region that were brought by conquerors?

❺ How has your group adapted to new ideas and innovations brought by other cultures?

_____

_____

_____

_____

_____

_____

_____

_____

_____

_____

_____

_____

© Harcourt

Name _____ Date _____

Present-Day Concerns

Directions Almanacs are sources of information about all the countries of the world. People use almanacs because they contain the most current information about governments, culture, and history. People also use almanacs for up-to-date information about countries' economies. Use the almanac information below to help you answer the questions about Morocco's economy.

Population: over 30 million people

Labor Force: 11 Million

Percentage of agricultural workers: 50%

Percentage of industrial and service workers: 45%

Industrial and Service Products: Phosphates, foods, leather, and textiles; tourism and construction

Agricultural Products: Barley, wheat, citrus, wine, vegetables, olives, and livestock

Area: 172,413 sq. miles or 446,515 sq. km

Trading Partners: France, Germany, India, Italy, Japan, Spain, and the United States

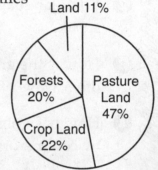

Land Use

Industrial Land 11%

Forests 20%

Pasture Land 47%

Crop Land 22%

1. What kinds of jobs do most of Morocco's workers have?

_____

2. What kinds of products do these Moroccan workers produce?

_____

3. Study the land use graph. How much land is used to produce these

products? _____

4. How would you describe the economy of Morocco? _____

_____

_____

_____

Use after reading Chapter 12, Lesson 4, pages 422–427.

© Harcourt

Name _____ Date _____

North Africa

Directions Complete this graphic organizer to show that you understand how to sequence events in the history of Egypt.

FIRST ➔ NEXT ➔ LAST

In 525 B.C. Persians conquer Egypt and rule it for 200 years.

⬇

In 332 B.C. Alexander the Great conquers Egypt.

⬇

About 31 B.C. _____

⬇

In A.D. 395 _____

About A.D. 643 _____

⬇

In A.D. 1798 the French take control of Egypt.

⬇

In the early A.D. 1800s Britain gains control of Egypt.

⬇

In A.D. 1922 _____

© Harcourt

Name _____ Date _____

12 Test Preparation

Directions Read each question and choose the best answer. Then fill in the circle for the answer you have chosen. Be sure to fill in the circle completely.

1 Most of the people in North Africa live in the—
- Ⓐ Coastal Plains.
- Ⓑ Tell Atlas.
- Ⓒ Sahara.
- Ⓓ Libyan Desert.

2 How does the Suez Canal benefit the people of North Africa and the world?
- Ⓕ It provides fresh drinking water to the Libyan coast.
- Ⓖ It links the Nile River to the Red Sea.
- Ⓗ It helps ships travel from the Mediterranean Sea to the Indian Ocean without going around Africa.
- Ⓙ It helps ships avoid the Nile cataracts and reach Lake Victoria in East Africa.

3 People flocked to North Africa's cities in modern times—
- Ⓐ to find small apartments.
- Ⓑ to find jobs or an education.
- Ⓒ to live on rooftops or boats.
- Ⓓ to preach Christianity.

4 What effect did the European conquest have on North Africa's countries?
- Ⓕ Europeans introduced Arabic laws and traditions into North Africa.
- Ⓖ Europeans influenced the laws and legal traditions of North Africa.
- Ⓗ Conquest helped the North Africans discover oil.
- Ⓙ The Europeans brought Islam into North Africa.

5 Which is one reason why European countries are North Africa's main trading partners?
- Ⓐ North African countries are colonies of European countries.
- Ⓑ North African goods are inexpensive.
- Ⓒ The European countries are very close to North Africa.
- Ⓓ Both Europeans and North Africans are Muslims.

Use after reading Chapter 12, pages 398–429.

Desert, Savanna, and Rain Forest

The three climate and vegetation regions in West and Central Africa have shaped the economies of the region's countries. The Sahel is an almost lifeless plain of sand dunes and gravel that borders the Sahara Desert in the north. The Sahel has little rainfall and long periods of drought. Few people live in this region. Its farmers grow dry-climate crops such as peanuts, cotton, millet, and sorghum. To the south of the Sahel is the savanna region. This is a region of flat plains and tall grasses. During the rainy season, farmers of the savanna grow such crops as potatoes, onions, corn, and yams. Large plantations in the savanna also grow such crops as coffee and cacao beans to be sold on the world market. Further south are the hot and wet rain forests. This region is the site of dense forests with few farms. Lumber, minerals, rubber, fruits, and fossil fuels are produced in this region.

Countries and Products of West and Central Africa			
Countries	**Products**	**Countries**	**Products**
Benin	beans, cassava, corn, cotton, rice, sorghum, palm products, peanuts, and petroleum	Burkina Faso	cattle, corn, cotton, goats, millet, peanuts, petroleum, rice, shea nuts, sheep, and sorghum
Cameroon	bananas, cassava, cocoa, coffee, cotton, millet, palm products, peanuts, petroleum, plantains, rubber, sorghum, tobacco, and yams	Chad	cassava, cotton, millet, peanuts, rice, sorghum, and yams
Democratic Republic of the Congo	cassava, coffee, corn, cotton, palm products, plantains, rice, rubber, tea, sugarcane, and yams	Gabon	cocoa, petroleum, and woods (okume, mahogany, ebony)
Mali	cassava, corn, cotton, millet, peanuts, rice, and sorghum	Niger	camels, cassava, cattle, cotton, cow peas, goats, millet, onions, peanuts, poultry, rice, sheep, and sorghum

(continued)

Name _____ Date _____

Directions Use the table on page 119 to help you identify the correct African country for each numbered item. Fill in the name of the country on the line provided.

1 Cocoa, coffee, cotton, and petroleum are four of the many products this Central African country produces. This country is called

_____ .

2 The country of _____ produces many subsistence crops, such as millet, cassava, and rice. The people of this country also raise goats, sheep, and camels.

3 Millet, cotton, peanuts, sorghum and other dry-climate crops are grown in

_____ and _____ ,

two West African countries located in the Sahel.

4 Sugarcane is a product of _____ , a large Central African country.

5 Woods and petroleum are major products of _____ .

6 The country of _____ produces many products, including shea nuts, livestock, and petroleum.

Directions Study the crops and minerals produced in each country. Use the information to help you choose the correct climate and vegetation region found in each country.

7 Exotic woods, cacao, and petroleum are found in Gabon. What type of climate and

vegetation region is located in Gabon? _____

8 Niger has two climate and vegetation regions where crops such as millet, peanuts, potatoes, and onions are grown. What kinds of regions are located in Niger?

_____

© Harcourt

Use after reading Chapter 13, Lesson 1, pages 444–449.

Name _____ Date _____

MAP AND GLOBE SKILLS
Compare Map Projections

Directions Read the paragraph and study the map projections below. Use the maps and your textbook to help you answer the questions that follow.

   Mapmakers, or cartographers, have developed several ways to show the round Earth on flat maps. These different ways are called projections. Each projection has its own distortions of the landforms and bodies of water on Earth. Equal-area projection maps show correct sizes of landforms, but the shapes are distorted. Conformal projection maps show directions correctly but alter the sizes of landforms and bodies of water. Cartographers think about these distortions when choosing maps for certain purposes.

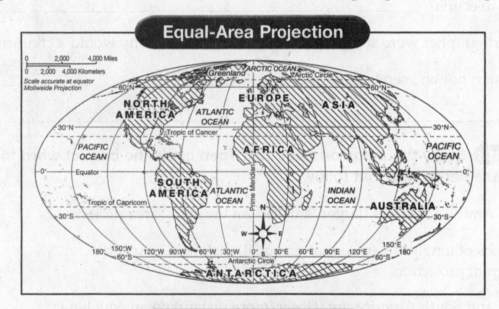

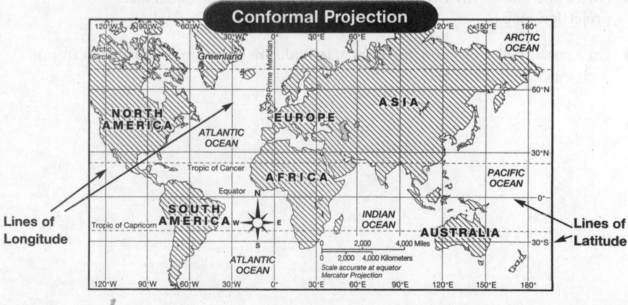

© Harcourt

(continued)

1 Which map projection would a cartographer use to study the shape of Africa?

_____

2 Which projection might be used to study the correct size of Antarctica?

_____

3 Which map projection might be used to determine the direction of Africa from

South America? _____

4 To compare the sizes of Madagascar and Iceland, a cartographer might use which

map projection? _____

5 If a cartographer were studying the size of Greenland, why would a conformal

projection not be used? _____

_____

Directions Study the maps on page 121. Then circle the correct word to complete the sentences that follow.

6 North America appears (larger/smaller) on the equal-area projection.

7 The lines of longitude are (equal/unequal) distances apart on a conformal projection.

8 Africa and South America are (closer/more distant) on an equal-area projection map.

9 On a conformal projection, the lines of latitude are (closer to/more distant from) each other near the poles.

© Harcourt

Use after reading Chapter 13, Skill Lesson, pages 450–451.

Name _____   Date _____

A Time of Empires

Directions West Africa has been the location of many powerful empires. Read the paragraph and study the map to help you answer the questions that follow.

The West African empires of Ghana, Mali, and Songhai controlled an area of busy trade routes. As the empires grew, they captured the trading cities located between West Africa and the Mediterranean region. Cities such as Timbuktu, Jenné, and Walata grew rich from the exchange of gold, salt, and slaves. In the busy markets of these cities, caravans carrying salt from North Africa traded their goods for the gold and other products of West Africa's coastal regions.

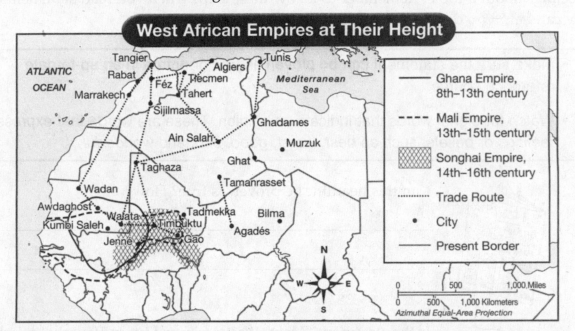

1 Which empire was established first and at its height controlled the cities of Walata and Kumbi Saleh? _____

2 Which empire rose to power as the empire of Ghana crumbled? _____

3 If a caravan left Tangier and traveled due south to Jenné, which cities would it have passed through on the journey? _____

4 Which empire was the larger in land area, Ghana or Mali?

_____

5 A caravan passing through the city of Timbuktu in the year 1320 would have been visiting which empire? _____

© Harcourt

Name _____   Date _____

READING SKILLS

Identify Fact and Opinion

Directions Read the tips for identifying facts and opinions. Then use the tips to help answer the questions that follow.

Every day we read facts and opinions in newspapers, books, and on the Internet. Identifying facts and opinions can sometimes be difficult. Facts are statements that can be proven as true. An opinion is a statement that expresses someone's belief or feelings about a topic. Remember to follow these steps when you read statements. They can help you decide if a statement is a fact or an opinion.

- Make sure the statement can be proven as true or untrue in an up-to-date reference source.

- Watch for signal words that indicate an opinion. These are words that express feelings or beliefs, such as *best, worst, good, bad,* and *wonderful.*

---

1  Can this headline be proven as true? How?

_____

_____

2  Is the statement "Many West Africans Live in Poverty" a fact or an opinion? How do you know?

_____

_____

3 How do you know this statement is an opinion and not a fact?

_____

_____

© Harcourt

Use after reading Chapter 13, Skill Lesson, pages 458–459.

Many Cultures

Directions Read the passages about African culture below. Then paraphrase, or write in your own words, the main idea of each passage.

1 Historians believe that groups of West African farmers speaking a language called Bantu migrated throughout West and Central Africa. As the farmers moved into new areas, they spread their language, agriculture, and tools. The languages of people in West and Central Africa have many similarities. Today, many of these languages continue to have several of the same words.

_____

_____

_____

2 Many African countries are home to many different ethnic groups. These countries' ethnic groups each have distinct languages. It is possible for African countries to have dozens of different languages spoken within their borders. The people in these countries also speak European languages introduced during the colonial period. All the ethnic groups in these countries speak a European language. The European languages are often the countries' official languages.

_____

_____

_____

3 In Chad and Mauritania, European languages are not official languages. Arab traders first reached these countries in the 700s. They spread Islam and the Arabic language to West Africa. Today, many African Muslims in Chad and Mauritania learn Arabic as part of their religious education. Arabic is an official language in

both countries. _____

_____

4 Many African languages are spoken by small ethnic groups. Some groups have fewer than 1,000 people. As the people of these ethnic groups are entered into larger cultural groups, their languages change and disappear. Someday these languages

may disappear altogether. _____

_____

© Harcourt

Developing Nations

Directions Many African countries gained their independence from European colonial empires after World War II. The newly-independent countries were faced with many problems. Study the list of problems. Then match the problems to the colonial characteristics that caused them. Write the problems on the lines under the matching colonial characteristics.

African workers became economically dependent on European trade.	African governments became corrupt.
African countries lacked skilled workers and managers.	African countries were autocracies or were ruled by the military.
African countries were made up of many different ethnic groups that did not unite into a single nation.	African roads and railroads were in poor condition.
	African economies were based on exporting a single crop or product.

Colonial Characteristics

European colonists in Africa raised cash crops and mined minerals for sale in Europe.

_____

_____

_____

_____

_____

_____

_____

_____

Colonial governments did little to train the Africans for independence.

_____

_____

_____

_____

_____

_____

_____

_____

© Harcourt

Use after reading Chapter 13, Lesson 4, pages 468–473.

Name _____ Date _____

West and Central Africa

Directions Complete this graphic organizer to show that you understand how to summarize key points about West and Central Africa.

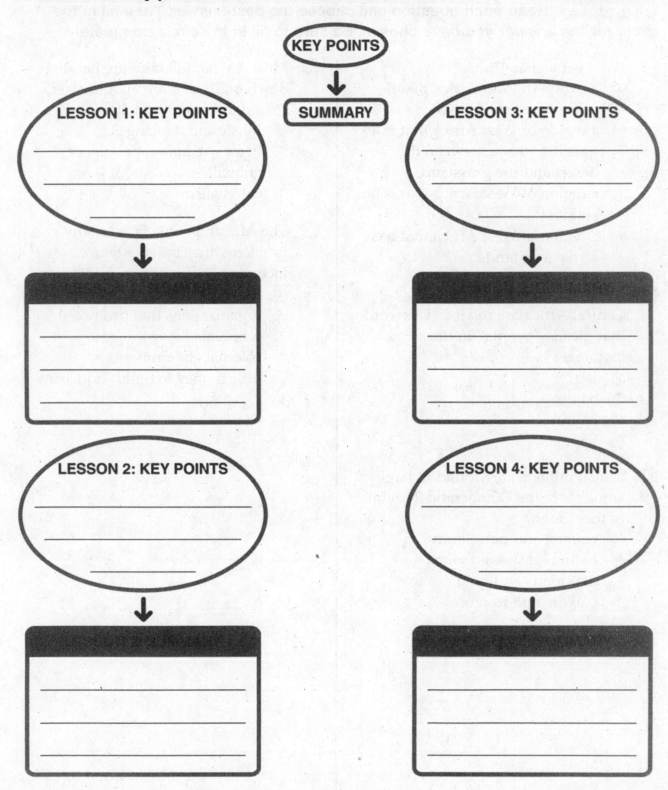

13 Test Preparation

Name _____ Date _____

Directions Read each question and choose the best answer. Then fill in the circle for the answer you have chosen. Be sure to fill in the circle completely.

1 What is the Sahel?
- Ⓐ a region of West Africa that lies next to the rain forests
- Ⓑ a region of West Africa that is a transition zone between the desert and the grasslands
- Ⓒ a region of West Africa that is hot 'and wet
- Ⓓ a region of West Africa that has fertile farmlands

2 Many languages in West and Central Africa are related. The word that means "people" in these languages is—
- Ⓕ twi.
- Ⓖ bantu.
- Ⓗ hausa.
- Ⓙ lingala.

3 Which minerals are found in large amounts in the Democratic Republic of the Congo?
- Ⓐ bauxite and petroleum
- Ⓑ natural gases and zinc
- Ⓒ diamonds and gold
- Ⓓ bauxite and iron ore

4 Most African folktales are handed down orally and are about—
- Ⓕ singers and storytellers.
- Ⓖ music and dancing.
- Ⓗ heroes, common people, or animals.
- Ⓙ colonialism.

5 The African people faced many problems after independence, including—
- Ⓐ the Organization of African Unity.
- Ⓑ organizations that promoted economic development.
- Ⓒ colonial governments.
- Ⓓ little money to build industries.

Use after reading Chapter 13, pages 442–475.

Plains and Plateaus

Directions Study the map of East and Southern Africa. Note the locations of the region's deserts, mountains, lakes, and rivers. Use the map to help you answer the questions on page 130.

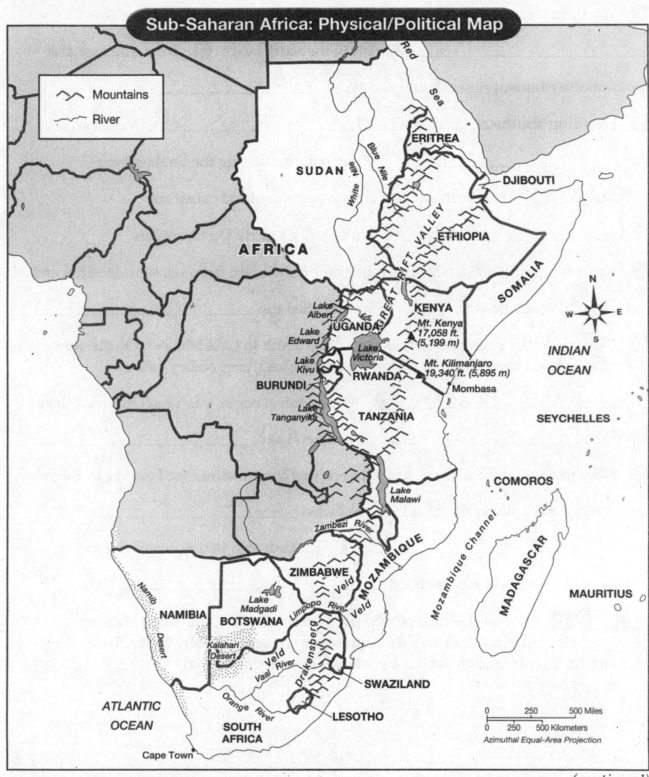

Sub-Saharan Africa: Physical/Political Map

(continued)

Name _____ Date _____

Directions To many explorers Africa seemed like a mysterious continent. High cliffs, deep lakes, and vast grasslands challenged early explorers. Now it is your turn to travel this vast continent and study its unique geography. Read the paragraph below and fill in the missing places. Use the map on page 129 and your textbook to help you complete the trip.

1 Start your trip in Cape Town, South Africa. Head to the almost waterless

_____ Desert in the northwest. **2** Turn due east and

cross another famous desert known as the _____.

3 Heading southeast, cross the _____ River and

the _____ River before reaching the Drakensberg

Mountains. **4** Turn northeast and cross a vast grassland called the

_____ by South Africa's early Dutch settlers.

5 Continuing northeast, begin traveling along the coast. Between your location and

the island of Madagascar is a body of water called the _____.

6 Now circle northwest through Kenya, then south to Lake Malawi. On the way, cross
the mountainous terrain that is part of eastern Africa's large valley called

_____. **7** As you travel north, you reach two more lakes,

Lake _____ and then Lake _____.

8 Now move to the east and pass between two large mountains. Looking through

your guidebook, you realize that they are called _____

and _____. **9** End your trip in the coastal city to the

southeast. This famous city is called _____.

Directions Review the completed paragraph above. On a separate sheet of paper, describe another trip through southern and eastern Africa. Have a classmate travel through Africa by following your directions.

Use after reading Chapter 14, Lesson 1, pages 478–484.

Name _____ Date _____

Ancient Cultures

Directions Powerful kingdoms and centers of trade grew up in East and Southern Africa. Study the pictures and read each of the facts concerning these civilizations. Decide which civilization each fact describes. Then write the name of the correct civilization on the line next to each fact.

Kingdom of Kush

Axumite Empire

The Great Zimbabwe

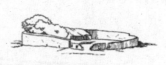
Swahili City-States

1 _____ An empire that was established on a plateau south of the Zambezi River. The capital of the empire was a large walled city.

2 _____ The empire expanded to include much of the Horn of Africa and even conquered Yemen on the Arabian Peninsula.

3 _____ The empire grew powerful by mining and trading the gold found in the region.

4 _____ The people of this empire were skilled ironworkers and had an agricultural industry that included cotton and flax.

5 _____ The empire converted to Christianity and became an important center of Christian learning.

6 _____ Arab merchants intermarried with Bantu peoples and established cities along the East African coast.

7 _____ Within the empire was a busy port named Adulis, where Africans traded ivory, gold, and slaves for Mediterranean wine, olive oil, iron, and brass tools.

8 _____ The merchants of this civilization traded with Arab merchants and the people of the African interior.

9 _____ The kingdom was influenced by the Egyptian civilization during its many years of close contact with the Egyptian Empire.

10 _____ The richest cities of this civilization, such as Dar es Salaam, had large mosques, palaces, and homes.

© Harcourt

Use after reading Chapter 14, Lesson 2, pages 485–491.

Activity Book ▪ 131

From Colonies to Countries

Directions Imagine that you are a newspaper reporter covering the struggle for freedom in Tanzania and South Africa. On a separate sheet of paper, write a short article that compares the independence movements in both countries. Include in your article the list of events and details below. Remember to start the article with an interesting headline and answer the questions Who? What? When? Where? and How?

South Africa

- Europeans, later known as Afrikaaners, settled South Africa in the seventeenth century.
- South Africa became part of Britain.
- In 1910, South Africa became independent of the British Empire.
- The African National Congress (ANC) fought to gain rights for Africans.
- In 1948, the National Party came to power and established apartheid.
- Violent protests by native Africans led the government to declare the ANC illegal.
- Nelson Mandela and other ANC leaders were arrested and imprisoned.
- From the mid 1970s until the late 1980s, other countries isolated South Africa.
- In 1989, South Africans voted to reform the government.
- In 1994, Nelson Mandela became the President of South Africa.

Tanzania

- Tanganyika had many European settlers.
- The colony had a well-organized nationalist movement headed by Julius Nyerere.
- Julius Nyerere united over 120 ethnic groups.
- The European settlers supported the country's new constitution.
- Tanganyika gained independence in 1958 and united with the island of Zanzibar in 1963.
- The two countries formed the new country of Tanzania.

Use after reading Chapter 14, Lesson 3, pages 492–498.

Facing the Future

Directions Political stability and economic independence are issues facing East and Southern Africa today. The information in this lesson is presented in four sections. Use your textbook to answer the question for each section.

Economic Development

1 How might the economies of the East and Southern African countries be

described? _____

_____

_____

Health and Welfare

2 Why do many East and Southern African countries have difficulty providing

health care and education to their citizens? _____

_____

_____

Protecting the Environment

3 How is deforestation changing the countries of East and Southern Africa?

_____

_____

Culture and Conflict

4 What problems arose in a country with more than one cultural group?

_____

_____

CHART AND GRAPH SKILLS
Compare Tables

Directions The tables below compare the populations, ethnic groups, dates of independence, and leaders for some countries in East and Southern Africa. Study the tables. Then answer the questions and complete the activities on the next page.

East Africa				
Country	Population	Ethnic Groups	Date of Independence	Heads of State
Djibouti	451,442	Afar, Arab, European, Somali	June 27, 1977	President and Prime Minister
Ethiopia	64,117,000	Afar, Amhara, Gurage, Oromo, Shankella, Sidamo, Somali, Tigre	Always Independent	President and Prime Minister
Uganda	23,317,560	Acholi, Arab, Asian, Baganda, Bagisu, Basogo, Batobo, Bunyoro, European, Karamojong, Langi, Lugbara, Rwanda	October 9, 1962	President
Somalia	7,253,137	Arab, Bantu, Somali	July 1, 1960	None

Southern Africa				
Country	Population	Ethnic Groups	Date of Independence	Heads of State
Botswana	1,576,470	Basarwa, Batswana, European, Kalanga, Kgalagadi	September 30, 1966	President
Lesotho	2,143,141	Asian, European, Sotho	October 4, 1966	King and President
Mozambique	19,104,696	Asian, Chokwe, European, Makua, Manyika, Shangaan, Sena	June 25, 1975	President and Prime Minister
Swaziland	1,083,289	European, Swazi, Shangaan, Tonga, Zulu	September 6, 1968	King and Prime Minister

© Harcourt

(continued)

Use after reading Chapter 14, Skill Lesson, pages 506–507.

Name _____ Date _____

1 Which of the countries in East and Southern Africa have kings?

_____

2 Which East or Southern African country has always been an independent nation?

_____

3 Which East or Southern African country has the largest population? Which

country has the smallest? _____

4 Name the East and Southern African countries that have both Presidents and

Prime Ministers leading their people. _____

5 Which Southern African countries have Shangaan people living within them?

_____

6 Which countries have Europeans as part of their populations?

_____

7 Which East or Southern African nation has no head of state?

_____

8 The Baganda, Bagisu, and Basogo people live in which country?

_____

Directions Use the tables to help you order the following lists. Write the
numbers 1–4 on the lines next to each country.

9 Countries by population
(Highest to Lowest)

_____ Botswana

_____ Somalia

_____ Mozambique

_____ Uganda

10 Countries by Date of Independence
(First to Last)

_____ Lesotho

_____ Djibouti

_____ Uganda

_____ Swaziland

© Harcourt

Name _____ Date _____

East and Southern Africa

Directions Complete this graphic organizer to show that you understand how to use facts and details to make generalizations about East Africa and Southern Africa.

FACTS + DETAILS		GENERALIZATION

Many East and Southern African countries have weak economies. They must deal with ethnic conflicts, famine, disease, and large amounts of foreign debt. Also, protecting the environment is a major concern.

_____
_____
_____
_____
_____

People from the many different world regions, including the Arabian peninsula and Europe, have settled in Africa. Each group brought with it new cultural ideas and influences, such as languages, religions, and customs.

_____
_____
_____
_____

© Harcourt

Use after reading Chapter 14, pages 476–509.

Name _____ Date _____

14 Test Preparation

Directions Read each question and choose the best answer. Then fill in the circle for the answer you have chosen. Be sure to fill in the circle completely.

1 The tall, steep cliffs that lie along Africa's east coast are called—
- Ⓐ rifts.
- Ⓑ grasslands.
- Ⓒ escarpments.
- Ⓓ pans.

2 The Afrikaaners are descendants of which people who settled in South Africa during the seventeenth century?
- Ⓕ Khoisan
- Ⓖ Portuguese
- Ⓗ English
- Ⓙ Dutch, French, and German

3 Why are many of the East African Lakes known as "Soda Lakes"?
- Ⓐ The lakes are full of salt water.
- Ⓑ The lakes are full of acid water.
- Ⓒ The lake water is neither fresh nor salt water, but alkaline.
- Ⓓ The lakes are drying up and losing water.

4 The South African policy of apartheid was designed to—
- Ⓕ keep people of European descent in control of the government and separate all the country's racial groups.
- Ⓖ establish a country of equal people regardless of race.
- Ⓗ keep the country as a British colony.
- Ⓙ recognize the African National Congress Party as a political party.

5 Many African nations are burdened with foreign debt. What is one solution that may solve the debt problem?
- Ⓐ The UN and other world organizations could stop lending money to African countries.
- Ⓑ The African countries could give foreign aid money to their leaders.
- Ⓒ The foreign debt could be canceled or repayment postponed.
- Ⓓ The UN could pay off the debt.

Use after reading Chapter 14, pages 476–509.

© Harcourt

Great Rivers, Mighty Monsoons

Directions South Asia has many different landforms and bodies of water. Study the map of the region, and label each landform and body of water. Use the clues below and your textbook to help you complete the activity.

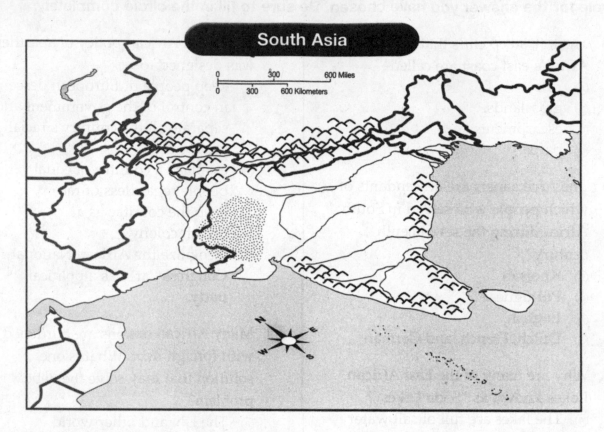

1 A massive mountain range with 95 peaks

_____

2 A body of water that is located along the eastern edge of the Indian subcontinent

_____

3 A high, flat area in the center of the Indian subcontinent; where most of the region's minerals are found

_____

4 A hot, dry region bordering the Ganges Plain and the Himalayas

_____

5 A large river and source of irrigation for the farmers of Pakistan

_____

© Harcourt

Use after reading Chapter 15, Lesson 1, pages 524–529.

Through the Ages

Directions Read the quotes below, which might have been said by South Asians at different times in history. Decide which group each speaker was talking about, select the name of that group from the box, and write it in the space provided. Use your textbook to help you complete the activity.

| Aryans   Moguls   People in Mohenjo-Daro   Mauryans   Arabs |

1 "They swept over the land from the north. They were nomads who had little use for our towns. Some of my people fled south. Some of us were captured and enslaved. Those of us who were captured were placed at the bottom of the social system. Nothing will ever be the same in the Indus Valley."

_____

2 "Like so many others before, these people came from the west and conquered Sind. These invaders saw our kingdoms at war and thought it was the best time to invade. They brought their religion with them. They call it Islam."

_____

3 "Our rulers are descendants of the great king Babur, who swept into India in 1526. Babur set up a beautiful capital city at Agra. Today our rulers are still descendants of Babur, but they take orders from the British. Our rulers always agree with them."

_____

4 "Our ruler Asoka is the third great king in the family. His father and grandfather both established our empire. At Perot, Asoka was ruthless. Now, however, he has embraced Buddhism."

_____

5 "My people have set up a wonderful city on the Indus River. Our city has wide streets and clay-brick homes. My home has a bathroom and plumbing. Next door is a shop where bread is baked. Far to the north is another city, called Harappa. I hear it is similar to my great city."

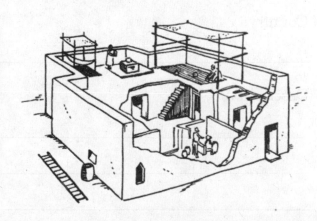

_____

People and Culture

Directions Study the pictures of the different styles of clothing worn in the countries of India, Nepal, Pakistan, and Sri Lanka. Next to each picture, write the name of the country in which it is worn and a description of the clothing.

Country:

Shawar Kameez

_____

Description:

_____

_____

_____

Country:

Dupatta

_____

Description:

_____

_____

_____

Country:

Sari

_____

Description:

_____

_____

_____

© Harcourt

Use after reading Chapter 15, Lesson 3, pages 536–540.

Name _____ Date _____

READING SKILLS
Predict a Likely Outcome

Directions You can use what you know about the history of a place or an event to help you predict what might happen in the future. Read the paragraph about Bangladesh, and then complete the questions below.

Until the eighteenth century, Bangladesh had many different Muslim and Hindu rulers. In 1757 Bangladesh became part of the British Empire in India. For the next 190 years the people of Bangladesh and other groups in India pressed the British for independence. When the British decided to give India its independence in 1947, they created two countries based on religion—Hindu India and Muslim Pakistan. The area now known as Bangladesh, with its many Muslim people, became a part of Pakistan called East Pakistan. As a result, Pakistan was a divided nation with its two halves widely separated. Over the next few decades, many people in East Pakistan felt that they had little in common with those in the west. The Bangladeshi people saw the western Pakistanis as just another group of foreign rulers.

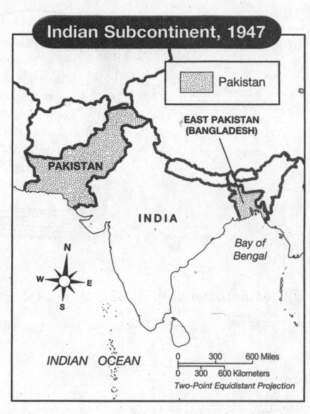

Indian Subcontinent, 1947

Pakistan

EAST PAKISTAN (BANGLADESH)

PAKISTAN

INDIA

Bay of Bengal

N W E S

INDIAN OCEAN

0   300   600 Miles
0   300   600 Kilometers
Two-Point Equidistant Projection

❶ What did you learn about Bangladesh? _____

_____

_____

_____

❷ What do you think happened to Pakistan's rule over Bangladesh?

_____

_____

_____

_____

© Harcourt

Name _____   Date _____

South Asia Today

Directions Read this diary entry, which might have been written by a student traveling in India. Then write your own series of short entries about each of the places listed below. Make sure you include the ideas described next to the name of each place. Use your textbook and other resources to help you complete the activity.

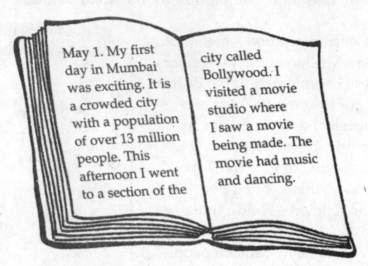

May 1. My first day in Mumbai was exciting. It is a crowded city with a population of over 13 million people. This afternoon I went to a section of the city called Bollywood. I visited a movie studio where I saw a movie being made. The movie had music and dancing.

1 Mumbai; museums and other places to see

May 2: _____

_____

2 A farming village; daily life of the people

May 6: _____

_____

3 Kolkata; poverty and living conditions

May 8: _____

_____

CHART AND GRAPH SKILLS

Read a Population Pyramid

Directions Look at the population pyramids on this page. They show the populations of Bangladesh and Italy. Compare the population patterns of these countries, and then answer the questions on page 144.

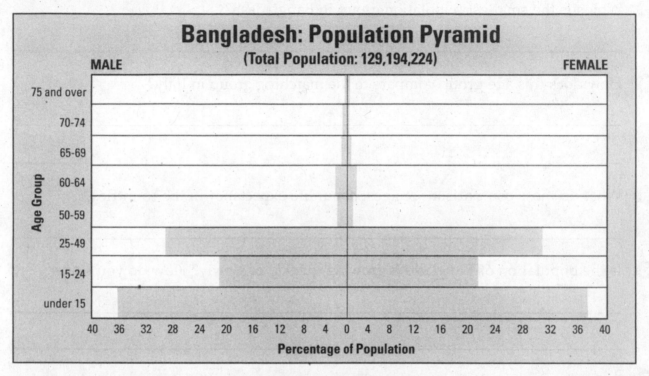

Bangladesh: Population Pyramid
(Total Population: 129,194,224)

MALE   FEMALE

Age Group: 75 and over, 70-74, 65-69, 60-64, 50-59, 25-49, 15-24, under 15

Percentage of Population: 40 36 32 28 24 20 16 12 8 4 0 4 8 12 16 20 24 28 32 36 40

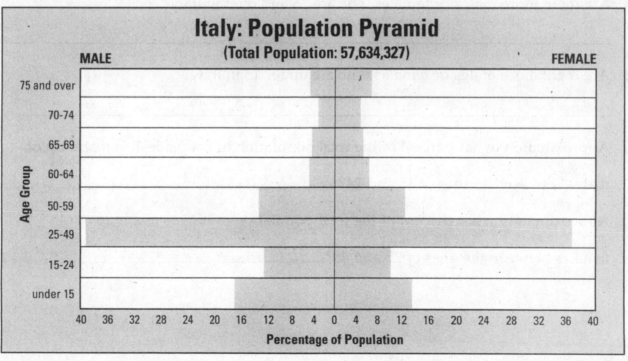

Italy: Population Pyramid
(Total Population: 57,634,327)

MALE   FEMALE

Age Group: 75 and over, 70-74, 65-69, 60-64, 50-59, 25-49, 15-24, under 15

Percentage of Population: 40 36 32 28 24 20 16 12 8 4 0 4 8 12 16 20 24 28 32 36 40

(continued)

© Harcourt

1 Which is the largest population group in Bangladesh? _____

_____

2 How does this age group compare to the matching group in Italy?

_____

3 Which is the smallest population group in Bangladesh? _____

_____

4 How does this age group compare to the matching group in Italy?

_____

_____

5 What do these comparisons suggest about life expectancy in the countries?

_____

6 Is the population of Bangladesh growing quickly or slowly? How do you know?

_____

_____

7 Are there more males or females who are 75 and over in Italy?

_____

8 Are there more males or females who are under 15 in Italy?

_____

9 Approximately what percent of the total population of Bangladesh is made up of

males between the ages of 15 and 24? _____

10 Approximately what percent of the total population of Italy is made up of

females between the ages of 25 and 49? _____

Use after reading Chapter 15, Skill Lesson, pages 548–549.

© Harcourt

South Asia

Directions Complete this graphic organizer to show that you understand how to write facts and opinions about South Asia.

TOPIC	FACT	OPINION
The Ganges River		
Sri Lanka		
Mohandas Gandhi		
Religions in South Asia		
India's Cities		
Clothing in South Asia		

© Harcourt

Use after reading Chapter 15, pages 522–551.

Name _____ Date _____

15 Test Preparation

Directions Read each question and choose the best answer. Then fill in the circle for the answer you have chosen. Be sure to fill in the circle completely.

1 The flat farmland in southern Nepal is called the—
- Ⓐ Kathmandu.
- Ⓑ Terai.
- Ⓒ Mount Everest Region.
- Ⓓ Duars Plains.

2 Monsoons bring warm, moist air and heavy rains to the region. If the rains come from the Indian Ocean, then which month of the year is it?
- Ⓕ November
- Ⓖ January
- Ⓗ April
- Ⓙ December

3 A religion that does not worship a god or supreme being is—
- Ⓐ Jainism.
- Ⓑ Hinduism.
- Ⓒ Islam.
- Ⓓ Sikhism.

4 What is the name of the land that India and Pakistan continue to fight over?
- Ⓕ Nepal
- Ⓖ Sri Lanka
- Ⓗ Kashmir
- Ⓙ the Maldives

5 In which South Asian country is the literacy rate 90 percent of the population?
- Ⓐ Pakistan
- Ⓑ Sri Lanka
- Ⓒ Nepal
- Ⓓ India

© Harcourt

Use after reading Chapter 15, pages 522–551.

Mountains, Deserts, Rivers, and Seas

Directions China can be described as a staircase with three separate steps. The highest step refers to the land in western China. The lowest step refers to the land along China's eastern coast. Read the list of physical and human features below. Fill in the chart by writing the features on the correct "steps". Use your textbook and the chart to help you answer the question that follows.

Features:

Plateau of Tibet	largest cities
source of the Huang He	coastline
source of the Chang Jiang	Northern Plateau
most productive farmland	Himalayas
largest population	source of the Xi River
Gobi (desert)	loess found in the Huang He

Steps:

West

Central

East

Why do you think most of the people in China live in the eastern part of the country? Continue on another sheet of paper if necessary.

_____

_____

_____

© Harcourt

Long-Lasting Civilizations

Directions China has been the location of many empires—from the empire of the Shang Dynasty to the Manchus. Each empire had an effect on the culture and history of East Asia. Fill in the missing information about each of the Chinese ruling dynasties.

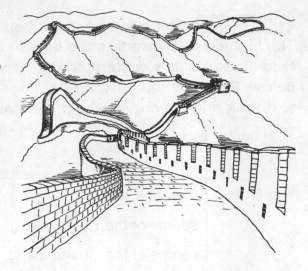

Shang Dynasty

• China's first dynasty

Zhou Dynasty

_____

_____

Qin Dynasty

_____

_____

Han Dynasty

_____

_____

_____

Mongols

• Traded goods such as silk, jewels, and porcelain with Marco Polo and Europe
• Controlled a vast empire that stretched to eastern Europe

Ming Dynasty

_____

_____

Qing Dynasty

• Established a peaceful empire
• Allowed much of China to fall under European influence

© Harcourt

Name _____ Date _____

CHART AND GRAPH SKILLS
Read a Cartogram

Directions A population cartogram shows countries based on the number of people that live there. Countries with larger populations are shown larger than countries that have smaller populations. Study the population cartogram below. Then use it to complete the activities.

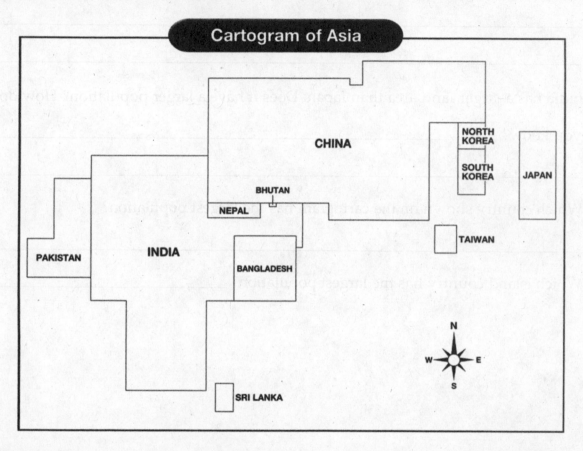

Cartogram of Asia

CHINA

NORTH KOREA

SOUTH KOREA

JAPAN

BHUTAN

NEPAL

TAIWAN

PAKISTAN

INDIA

BANGLADESH

SRI LANKA

N
W   E
S

Directions Review the population cartogram above. Then order the following countries by population, starting with 1 for the country with the largest population.

_____ North Korea    _____ Bhutan

_____ India    _____ China

_____ Pakistan   _____ Japan

(continued)

Name _____ Date _____

Directions Use the population cartogram on page 149 to answer the following questions about countries in East Asia.

1 Which country has a larger population, Bangladesh or South Korea?

_____

2 How can you tell which of the two nations has a larger population?

_____

_____

3 India has a larger land area than Japan. Does it have a larger population? How do

you know? _____

_____

4 Which country shown on the cartogram has the largest population?

_____

5 Which island country has the largest population? _____

Use after reading Chapter 16, Skill Lesson, pages 568–569.

A Life of Traditions and Religions

Directions The teachings of Confucius are still popular around the world. Read the sayings of Confucius that are listed below. Then on the blank scroll, write your own Confucian saying about each of the topics. Share your sayings with the class.

Education

To eat your fill but not apply your mind to anything all day is a problem.

Good Manners

Good people bring out what is good in others, not what is bad.

Respect Others

Do not do to others what you would not want yourself.

Respect and Honor Parents

A young man's duty is to behave well to his parents at home and to his elders abroad.

_____

_____

_____

_____

_____

_____

_____

_____

A Region of Contrasts

Directions Read the statements about the economies of the East Asian countries. Decide if each statement is true or false. In the space provided, write *T* if it is true or *F* if it is false. Use your textbook if necessary.

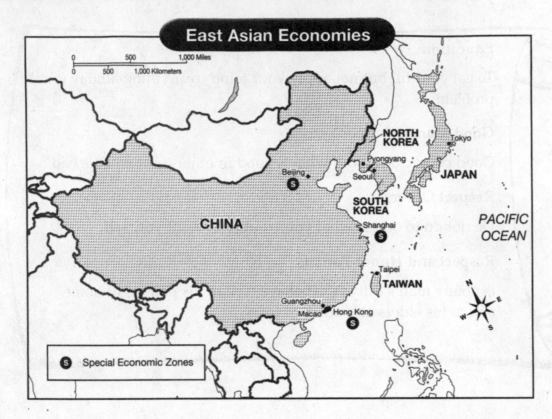

East Asian Economies

1 _____ China's economy is based on a system called keiretsu, in which companies maintain strong ties with each other.

2 _____ South Korea exports minerals and metal products.

3 _____ Japan has strengthened the economies of many other East Asian countries by investing in them.

4 _____ The city of P'yongyang is a Special Economic Zone.

5 _____ Japan is a country that imports raw materials to create products for export.

6 _____ The economy of North Korea is far behind the economies of the rest of East Asia.

7 _____ The city of Hong Kong is a Special Economic Zone.

8 _____ China's Special Economic Zones are along its eastern coast.

© Harcourt

Use after reading Chapter 16, Lesson 4, pages 575–579.

Name _____ Date _____

East Asia

Directions Complete this graphic organizer to show that you understand how to draw conclusions about East Asia.

WHAT YOU READ	+	WHAT YOU KNOW	→	CONCLUSION

The Pacific Ocean provides the countries of East Asia with many benefits, such as fishing and routes for trading and transportation. However, monsoons bring heavy rains in the summer and strong winds in the winter. Parts of East Asia are on the Ring of Fire and are prone to volcanic eruptions, earthquakes, and tsunamis.

_____
_____
_____
_____
_____
_____

_____
_____
_____
_____
_____
_____

_____
_____
_____
_____
_____
_____

The ideas of philosophers and thinkers often have an influence on culture. Confucius had a lot of sayings people still refer to today. Religion plays an important part in the lives of many people around the world.

_____
_____
_____
_____
_____
_____

© Harcourt

Name _____   Date _____

16 Test Preparation

Directions Read each question and choose the best answer. Then fill in the circle for the answer you have chosen. Be sure to fill in the circle completely.

1 Earth's tallest mountain range is called the—
- Ⓐ Takla Makan.
- Ⓑ Himalayas.
- Ⓒ Top of the World.
- Ⓓ Gobi.

2 The Japanese islands are—
- Ⓕ the peaks of a long underwater mountain range.
- Ⓖ made up of coral and sand.
- Ⓗ covered with flat farmlands.
- Ⓙ not affected by the winds that blow over the water.

3 The _____ Dynasty of China expanded the country's borders and spread Chinese culture to Korea and Japan.
- Ⓐ Qing
- Ⓑ Han
- Ⓒ Manchu
- Ⓓ Zhou

4 Which teaching or religion stressed a simple life in harmony with nature?
- Ⓕ Confucianism
- Ⓖ Shintoism
- Ⓗ Daoism
- Ⓙ Buddhism

5 Japan's economy is—
- Ⓐ based on exporting high-quality manufactured products.
- Ⓑ based on exporting minerals and fossil fuels.
- Ⓒ not successful compared to other countries in East Asia.
- Ⓓ a command economy.

Use after reading Chapter 16, pages 552–581.

Peninsulas, Islands, and Seas

Directions Be a cartographer. Create your own map of mainland Southeast Asia. First, study the map on page 585 of your textbook. Then answer the questions below. Next, draw the map in the space provided. Include on your map the answers to the questions.

1 What countries are located on the mainland of Southeast Asia?

_____

2 What is the peninsula on which five of the mainland countries are located?

_____

3 What is the peninsula on which Malaysia and part of Thailand are located?

_____

4 What river flows through Laos, Thailand, Cambodia, and southern Vietnam?

_____

5 Which strait and large sea separate the mainland of Southeast Asia from the island

countries of the region? _____

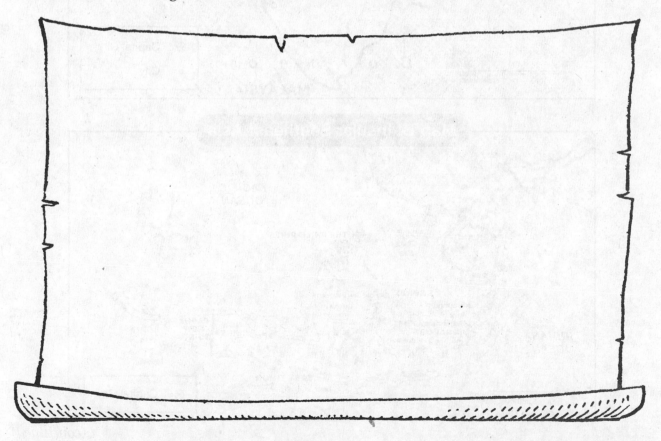

MAP AND GLOBE SKILLS

Compare Maps of Different Scale

Directions Map scales compare the distances on maps with the actual distances. Study these maps, and answer the questions that follow.

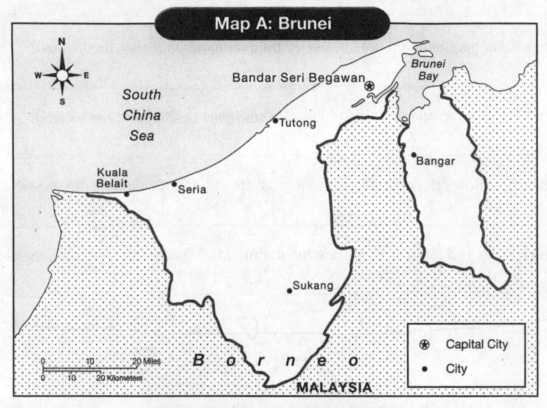

Map A: Brunei

N W E S

South China Sea

Bandar Seri Begawan

Brunei Bay

•Tutong

•Bangar

Kuala Belait

•Seria

•Sukang

0 10 20 Miles
0 10 20 Kilometers

B o r n e o

MALAYSIA

⊛ Capital City
• City

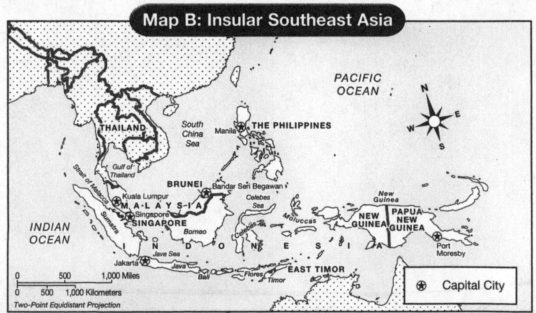

Map B: Insular Southeast Asia

PACIFIC OCEAN

THAILAND

South China Sea

Manila • **THE PHILIPPINES**

N W E S

Gulf of Thailand

Strait of Malacca

BRUNEI ⊛Bandar Seri Begawan

Celebes Sea

New Guinea

PAPUA NEW GUINEA

Kuala Lumpur ⊛
M A L A Y S I A
⊛Singapore
SINGAPORE

Sumatra

Borneo

NEW GUINEA ⊛

Moluccas

Celebes

INDIAN OCEAN

I N D O N E S I A

Port Moresby ⊛

Jakarta •
Java Sea
Java *Bali* *Flores* **EAST TIMOR**
Timor

0 500 1,000 Miles
0 500 1,000 Kilometers
Two-Point Equidistant Projection

⊛ Capital City

(continued)

Use after reading Chapter 17, Skill Lesson, pages 590–591.

© Harcourt

1 Which map shows the country of Brunei in more detail? _____

2 Which map would you use to find the distance between the cities of Jakarta and

Bandar Seri Begawan? _____

3 In which country is the city of Tutong located? _____

4 On which map did you find the city of Tutong? Explain why you chose that map.

_____

_____

_____

5 Which map shows a larger area of Southeast Asia? Why? _____

_____

_____

_____

Directions **Study the scales of the two maps on page 156, then answer the questions below.**

6 Which city is farther from Manila—Jakarta or Port Moresby?

_____

7 How many miles apart are the cities Bandar Seri Begawan and Tutong?

_____

8 How many miles apart are the cities Singapore and Jakarta?

_____

9 How far apart are the two parts of Malaysia? _____

_____

10 Which islands are closer to each other—the islands Java and Timor or the islands

New Guinea and Borneo? _____

_____

Name _____ Date _____

In the Shadow of Others

Directions An outline is a list of important ideas that organize information about a topic. An outline shows you how important ideas relate to one another. The history of Southeast Asia is a large topic. Study the outline below of the region's history. Use your textbook to help you fill in the missing information.

I. Early Cultures and Kingdoms
   A. Different Ethnic Groups

     1. People from China migrated south to the region.

     2. _____

     _____

   B. Early Kingdoms

     1. The Mons established the Kingdom of Funan in the first century A.D.

     2. _____

     _____

     3. The Malay people of Sumatra established a Buddhist kingdom called Srivijaya that lasted until A.D. 1290.

II. New Arrivals to the Region
   A. New Ethnic Groups and Religions

     1. Thai people arrived in the 1200s and began to establish powerful kingdoms.

     2. _____

   B. The Europeans Arrive

     1. Starting in the 1500s, Portuguese, Dutch, Spanish, and English traders arrived.

     2. _____

III. World War II to Present
   A. World War II and Independence

     1. _____

     2. After World War II, many countries in the region began to win independence from the Europeans.

     3. Communist and non-communist groups struggled for power in many countries.

Use after reading Chapter 17, Lesson 2, pages 592–596.

Varying Economies, Varying Governments

Directions Both Brunei and Thailand have governments with monarchs. Compare these governments by studying the charts below. Then complete the statements below, underlining the correct term.

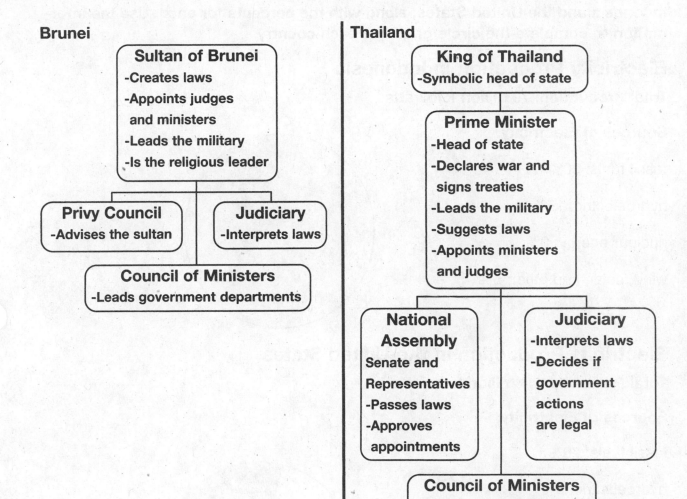

Brunei

Sultan of Brunei
-Creates laws
-Appoints judges and ministers
-Leads the military
-Is the religious leader

Privy Council
-Advises the sultan

Judiciary
-Interprets laws

Council of Ministers
-Leads government departments

Thailand

King of Thailand
-Symbolic head of state

Prime Minister
-Head of state
-Declares war and signs treaties
-Leads the military
-Suggests laws
-Appoints ministers and judges

National Assembly
Senate and Representatives
-Passes laws
-Approves appointments

Judiciary
-Interprets laws
-Decides if government actions are legal

Council of Ministers
-Recommends laws
-Runs the government

1 In Brunei the **(sultan/Privy Council)** is the head of state.

2 In Thailand the **(National Assembly/king)** and the **(prime minister/Council of Ministers)** are the heads of state.

3 In Thailand the **(Council of Ministers/National Assembly)** passes laws.

4 In Brunei, laws are created by the **(sultan/Council of Ministers)**.

5 In both countries the **(Judiciary/National Assembly)** interprets laws.

Name _____ Date _____

CHART AND GRAPH SKILLS
Compare Circle Graphs

Directions Electricity is an important form of energy in Southeast Asia as well as in the United States. Listed below are the sources of electricity in both Indonesia and the United States, along with the percents for each. Use the information to complete the circle graph for each country.

Electricity Production in Indonesia

Total Production: 79 billion kilowatts

Sources of Electricity:

fossil fuels: 80%

hydroelectric: 15%

nuclear energy: 0%

wind, solar, and other: 5%

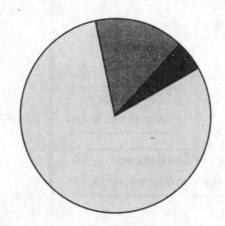

Electricity Production in the United States

Total Production: 4 trillion kilowatts

Sources of Electricity:

fossil fuels: 70%

hydroelectric: 8%

nuclear energy: 20%

wind, solar, and other: 2%

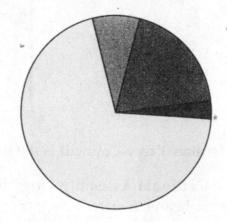

© Harcourt

(continued)

Use after reading Chapter 17, Skill Lesson, pages 602–603.

Name _____ Date _____

Directions Study the circle graphs on page 160. Use the graphs to answer the questions below.

1 Which country produces more kilowatts of electricity? _____

2 How many general sources of electricity does Indonesia have? Name the sources.

_____

_____

3 Which source of electricity is found in the United States but not in Indonesia?

_____

4 What is the largest source used to produce electricity in the United States?

_____

5 Three general sources of electricity are used in both Indonesia and the United States. Which of these three sources generates the smallest amount of electricity?

_____

6 What is the largest source used to produce electricity in Indonesia?

_____

7 Compare the percentages of electricity generated from hydroelectric sources in both countries. How much more electricity is generated in Indonesia from this source than

in the United States? _____

8 Which general energy source produces 5% of Indonesia's supply of electricity?

_____

9 Which do you think is easier to read, the list of sources of electricity or the circle graph?

Explain. _____

_____

Southeast Asia

Directions Complete this graphic organizer to show that you understand cause-and-effect relationships about Southeast Asia.

CAUSE	→	EFFECT

| | → | Many kinds of animals are now considered endangered or threatened in Southeast Asia. |

| Plates on Earth's surface in Southeast Asia continue to shift. | → | |

| | → | Laos has difficulty trading with countries other than its neighbors. |

| Past wars and political problems plague Vietnam. | → | |

Use after reading Chapter 17, pages 582–605.

© Harcourt

Name _____ Date _____

Test Preparation

Directions Read each question and choose the best answer. Then fill in the circle for the answer you have chosen. Be sure to fill in the circle completely.

1 A part of Southeast Asia made up of many islands is—
- Ⓐ Mainland Southeast Asia.
- Ⓑ Laos.
- Ⓒ Insular Southeast Asia.
- Ⓓ Isthmus of Kra.

2 The weather in Southeast Asia is almost always—
- Ⓕ neither hot nor cool.
- Ⓖ dry and hot.
- Ⓗ dry and cool.
- Ⓙ hot and humid.

3 The _____ Kingdom of Srivijaya took control of the trade that flowed between India and China.
- Ⓐ Malay
- Ⓑ Chinese
- Ⓒ Khmer
- Ⓓ Mon

4 The idea that country after country would be taken over by communists was known as the—
- Ⓕ protectorate.
- Ⓖ domino effect.
- Ⓗ East Indies effect.
- Ⓙ Southeast Asia plan

5 Which nation has a strong economy based mostly on the technology and banking industries but has almost no agriculture?
- Ⓐ Thailand
- Ⓑ Indonesia
- Ⓒ the Philippines
- Ⓓ Singapore

Name _____ Date _____

The Lands Down Under

Directions Australia and New Zealand have diverse climates, landforms, animals, and plant life. Compare the two countries by completing the chart. Fill in the boxes for each category with specific names or details. Use your textbook to help you complete the activity.

Australia   New Zealand

Climate

Landforms

Animals

Plants

© Harcourt

Use after reading Chapter 18, Lesson 1, pages 620–624.

Outposts in the Pacific

Directions The Aborigines of Australia and the Maori of New Zealand were the first inhabitants of these lands. Read the list of activities below. Then make a check mark to show which group might have performed each one.

	Aborigines	The Maori
1 Weave clothing from flax.	☐	☐
2 Tell dreamtime stories.	☐	☐
3 Make rock art.	☐	☐
4 Hunt birds, seals, and whales.	☐	☐
5 Make tools from rocks and wood.	☐	☐
6 Ask a neighboring tribe for permission to hunt on their land.	☐	☐
7 Carve a boomerang from a tree branch.	☐	☐
8 Build a large wooden canoe.	☐	☐
9 Move with the family to a different location in search of food.	☐	☐
10 Speak with wise tribal elders.	☐	☐

Directions Imagine you are a member of one of the groups above. Write about what a day in your life would be like.

_____

_____

_____

_____

_____

_____

© Harcourt

Use after reading Chapter 18, Lesson 2, pages 625–631.

Name _____   Date _____

CITIZENSHIP SKILLS

Act as a Responsible Citizen

Read about the problems Australians have with dingoes. Then state the problem and check off solutions that you think a responsible citizen might suggest. Make sure the solutions benefit the entire community.

Dingoes are wild dogs that first appeared in Australia thousands of years ago with Asian traders. The dogs spread quickly over the continent, hunting small mammals, reptiles, and birds. When the Europeans arrived, their sheep herds became another source of food for the dingoes. In 1960 the ranchers convinced the Australian government to build a fence to stop the dingoes from attacking their sheep. The fence stretches 3,307 miles from the state of South Australia to Queensland. Today the dingoes inside the fence are hunted by ranchers who want to protect their sheep. The dingoes on the outside of the fence live in barren lands with few sources of food. Some Australians are worried that the dingoes will be hunted or starved into extinction. They are also concerned that the populations of many other animals, such as the emu, are growing too large without the dingoes to keep them under control. Despite these protests the sheep ranchers and many other Australians are firm about keeping the dingoes outside the fence and want to continue hunting the dingoes that threaten their herds.

The Problem

_____

_____

_____

_____

❶ Inside the fenced area, set aside tracts of land where the dingoes can live and hunt the other animal species. ☐

❷ Stop hunting the dingoes and push all of them outside the fence. ☐

❸ Feed the dingoes on both sides of the fence and protect the sheep herds. ☐

❹ Allow the dingoes to feed on the sheep herds. ☐

❺ Continue pushing the dingoes outside the fence and hunting those found inside near the sheep herds. ☐

Australia and New Zealand Today

Directions Settlers in Australia introduced many new animals to the continent. Some had a devastating effect on the native plants and animals. Study the chart below that lists some of these animals and the effects they had on the continent. Then read each pair of statements. For each pair, place an X next to the statement that is supported by the information on the chart.

Animal	Reasons for Introduction	Results
Cat	• Pets • Control rodent population	• Destroy native rodents
Camel	• Desert transportation	• Form large wild herds
Cane toad	• Control insect population	• Multiply into large numbers • Become pests
Rabbit	• Sport hunting • Food	• Dig burrows that destroy vegetation and speed up desertification
Red fox	• Sport hunting • Control rabbit population	• Destroy rabbits and native marsupials

1 _____ Some animals were introduced to fill the barren land.

_____ Some animals were introduced to correct the problems that were caused by other animals.

2 _____ Rabbits were introduced to control insects.

_____ Rabbits were a source of food.

3 _____ The red fox was introduced for sport.

_____ The red fox was a solution to the cane toad problem.

4 _____ Cane toads and cats were introduced as pets.

_____ Cats were introduced as pets.

5 _____ Camels carried products and passengers across the barren outback.

_____ Camels are still a main source of transportation.

CHART AND GRAPH SKILLS
Compare Line Graphs

Directions Read the paragraph below and study the line graphs. Then use the graphs to complete the activity on page 169.

Imagine you are working for Australia's Census Bureau. The line graphs below show you some information about a fictional Australian town named Oolamago. The town's population has doubled several times since the year 1900. The first shows the growth of the town's native population between the years 1900 and 2000. The next is a double-line graph. It shows the town's population of people from other countries and from other parts of Australia.

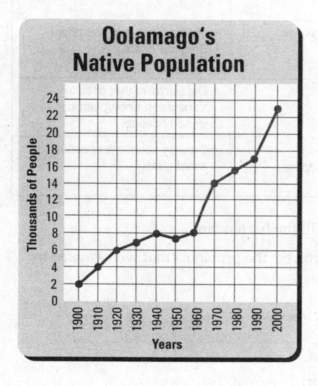

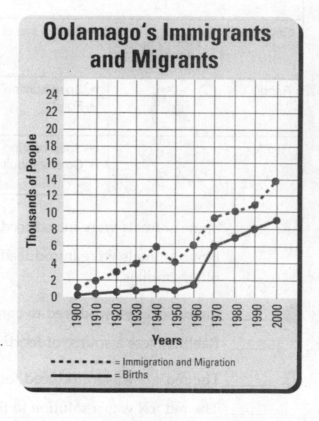

Use after reading Chapter 18, Skill Lesson, pages 640–641.

(continued)

© Harcourt

Name _____ Date _____

Directions The Census Bureau Chief has asked you to write a brief report analyzing Oolamago's population growth over the past century. Study the graphs on page 168. Then write your analysis following the outline below. Use a separate sheet of paper if you need more space.

I. Oolamago's Native Population from 1900–2000

    A. Growth between 1900 and 1940

    B. Decline between 1940 and 1950

    C. Rapid growth between 1960 and 1970

II. **Oolamago's Sources of Population Growth**

    A. Immigration

    B. Migration

_____

_____

_____

_____

_____

_____

_____

_____

_____

_____

_____

© Harcourt

Name _____ Date _____

Australia and New Zealand

Directions Complete this graphic organizer to show that you can use your knowledge about European settlement to make inferences about culture in Australia and New Zealand today.

DETAILS + KNOWLEDGE INFERENCE

DETAILS

KNOWLEDGE

People from Southeast Asia settled in Australia. They became known as Aborigines. They had no formal government, and they believed in dreamtime spirits. In New Zealand the first people came from Polynesia and called themselves the Maori. They formed tribes and honored gods of nature and their ancestors. Unlike the Aborigines, they were fierce warriors. In 1788 Britain began using Australia as a penal colony. Eventually, British colonists settled in Australia and New Zealand. Immigrants from around the world have also come to Australia and New Zealand.

_____
_____
_____
_____
_____
_____
_____
_____
_____
_____
_____
_____

INFERENCE

_____
_____

Use after reading Chapter 18, pages 618–643.

Name _____ Date _____

18 Test Preparation

Directions Read each question and choose the best answer. Then fill in the circle for the answer you have chosen. Be sure to fill in the circle completely.

1 The Murray and Darling Rivers flow through which Australian landform?
- Ⓐ the grasslands
- Ⓑ the outback
- Ⓒ the western plateau
- Ⓓ Pacific Ocean coast

2 Much of the world's _____ comes from northeastern Australia and is used to make aluminum.
- Ⓕ iron
- Ⓖ copper
- Ⓗ bauxite
- Ⓙ nickel

3 The first settlers of New Zealand are called the Maori. The name *Maori* means—
- Ⓐ "ancient ancestors."
- Ⓑ "Polynesian."
- Ⓒ "local people."
- Ⓓ "island settlers."

4 One of the most important and fastest growing industries in Australia and New Zealand is—
- Ⓕ sheep ranching.
- Ⓖ tourism.
- Ⓗ gold mining.
- Ⓙ lumbering.

5 What happened in 1972 that forced Australia and New Zealand to build stronger economic ties with each other?
- Ⓐ Asia wanted to develop trade with Australia.
- Ⓑ The United States increased its influence in the South Pacific.
- Ⓒ New Zealand's population increased.
- Ⓓ Britain joined the European Economic Community.

Name _____ Date _____

Island Migrations

Directions The islands of the Pacific can be classified into three regions—Melanesia, Micronesia, and Polynesia. Thousands of years ago cultures spread as people moved from island to island. Trace the routes of these people on the map below by following the instructions on page 173.

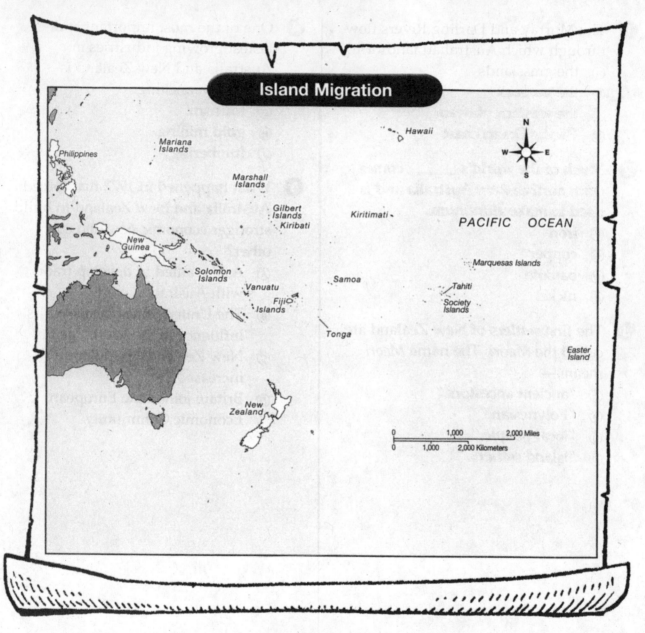

(continued)

Name _____ Date _____

Melanesians

1 Melanesian people moved from New Guinea to the Solomon Islands.

2 From the Solomon Islands, the Melanesians migrated to Vanuatu and the Fiji Islands.

Micronesians

3 People from the Philippines settled the Mariana Islands.

4 Micronesian people from New Guinea and the Solomon Islands sailed east and north to the Gilbert and Marshall Islands.

Polynesians

5 Polynesian people from the Fiji Islands moved to Tonga and Samoa.

6 From Tonga and Samoa, the Polynesians settled Tahiti and the Society Islands.

7 These Polynesians settled the Marquesas Islands to the northeast.

8 Polynesians migrated from the Marquesas Islands north to Hawaii.

9 Polynesians from the Marquesas Islands settled Easter Island.

10 Polynesians from the Marquesas Islands moved southwest to New Zealand.

Study the map. Which group settled the largest area of the Pacific Ocean? What effect do you think the group's migration had on the region?

_____

_____

_____

_____

© Harcourt

Name _____ Date _____

Island Nations

Directions There are different kinds of islands in the Pacific Ocean. Study the pictures of two types below. Use your textbook to help you identify the island types, and write their names on the lines provided. Then answer the questions that follow.

1 _____   **2** _____

3 Which kind of island was formed by an eruption that pushed a volcano above the

water? _____

4 Which kind of island was formed by thousands of small animals called coral that

attached themselves to a small piece of land? _____

5 Which kind of island has rich and fertile soils that can be used for agriculture?

_____

6 Which kind of island is more likely to have dense forests of beech and pine trees?

_____

7 Are forests more likely to grow on the eastern or western side of the islands'

mountains? _____

8 On which kind of island are palm trees found? _____

_____

9 Which kind of island is more likely to be inhabited and why?

_____

_____

Use after reading Chapter 19, Lesson 2, pages 654–659.

© Harcourt

Name _____ Date _____

MAP AND GLOBE SKILLS
Compare Different Kinds of Maps

Directions There are many kinds of maps. Each kind shows different information. It is important to learn how to read different maps and to relate them to each other. Study the maps below and on page 176 and use them to complete the activities that follow.

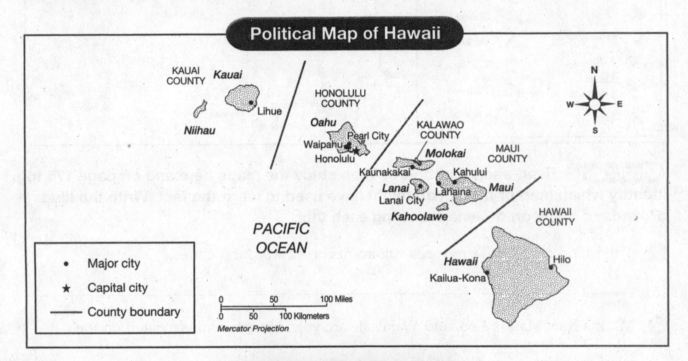

Political Map of Hawaii

KAUAI COUNTY — *Kauai*
Niihau — Lihue

HONOLULU COUNTY
Oahu
Waipahu — Pearl City
Honolulu

KALAWAO COUNTY
Molokai
Kaunakakai — Kahului
Lanai
Lanai City — Lahaina — *Maui*
Kahoolawe

MAUI COUNTY

HAWAII COUNTY
Hawaii
Kailua-Kona — Hilo

PACIFIC OCEAN

- Major city
★ Capital city
— County boundary

0   50   100 Miles
0   50   100 Kilometers
Mercator Projection

Physical Map of Hawaii

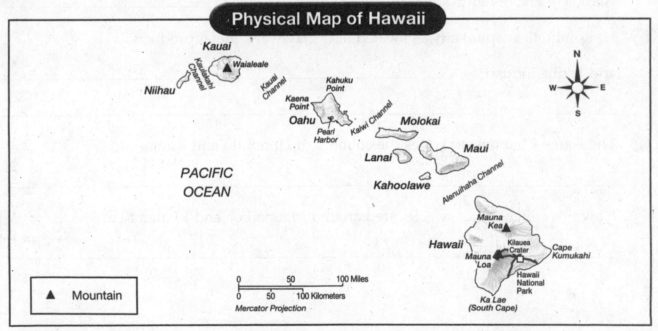

Kauai
Waialeale
Niihau — Kaulakahi Channel
Kauai Channel
Kahuku Point
Kaena Point
Oahu
Pearl Harbor
Kaiwi Channel
Molokai
Lanai
Maui
Kahoolawe
Alenuihaha Channel

PACIFIC OCEAN

Mauna Kea
Hawaii
Mauna Loa
Kilauea Crater
Cape Kumukahi
Hawaii National Park
Ka Lae (South Cape)

▲ Mountain

0   50   100 Miles
0   50   100 Kilometers
Mercator Projection

(continued)

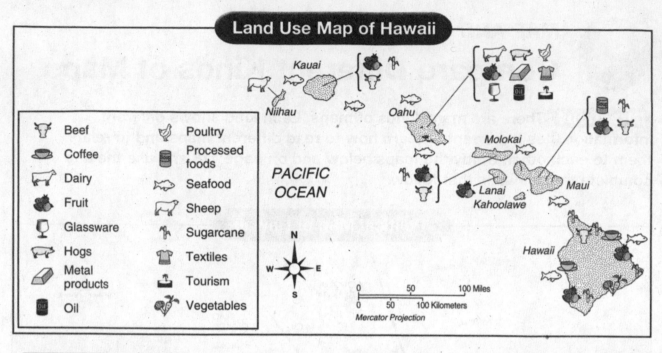

Land Use Map of Hawaii

Kauai

Niihau

Oahu

Molokai

PACIFIC
OCEAN

Lanai
Kahoolawe

Maui

Hawaii

Beef		Poultry	
Coffee		Processed foods	
Dairy		Seafood	
Fruit		Sheep	
Glassware		Sugarcane	
Hogs		Textiles	
Metal products		Tourism	
Oil		Vegetables	

N
W   E
S

0   50   100 Miles
0   50   100 Kilometers
Mercator Projection

Directions Read each fact below. Then study the maps here and on page 175 to identify which map or maps you might have used to learn the fact. Write the kind or kinds of maps on the line following each fact.

1 The island of Hawaii produces sugarcane, beef cattle, and coffee.

_____

2 Mauna Kea, Mauna Loa, and Waialeale are volcanic mountains located on the

islands of Hawaii and Kauai. _____

3 Honolulu, the capital city, is located near glassware, metal products,

and textile industries. _____

_____

4 The Kauai Channel separates the counties of Honolulu and Kauai.

_____

5 Hawaii's coffee industry is located around Mauna Loa and Mauna Kea.

_____

© Harcourt

Antarctica: A Continent Without a Population

Directions Antarctica is a land without a permanent population, but humans do visit the frozen continent. Many scientists and tourists go there to study the barren land. A tourist visiting Antarctica may have written the following letters. Read the letters and write one more, about the rest of the tourist's visit. You may want to use your textbook or other resource materials to provide details for your letter.

November 1

Dear Mom and Dad,

We just landed on Antarctica's Ross Island at McMurdo, one of three United States research bases. The base is much larger than I expected. It has an airport, fuel depots, dormitories, and even a library. Many people stop here on their way to the South Pole. It is very cold here. Someone told me that the average temperature is ⁻56°F, and I believe it. I am wearing many layers of clothes, heavy boots, and a parka. The sun is bright because of the glare that reflects off the snow. To protect my eyes, I am wearing goggles. The people at the base drive around in special vehicles that have tracks instead of tires. The tracks stop the vehicle from sliding, but they also make it move slowly. Today I am going for a ride to explore the area outside the base. I will write again soon.

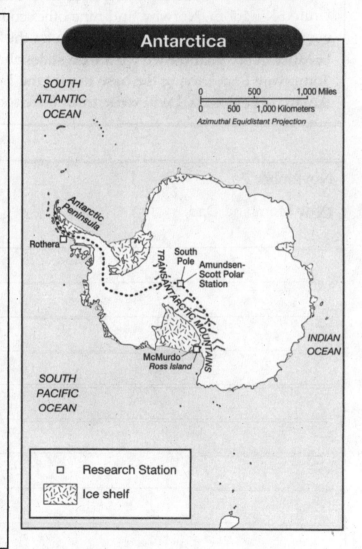

© Harcourt

(continued)

Name _____ Date _____

November 6

Dear Mom and Dad,

    I made it to the South Pole! I flew to the Amundsen-Scott Polar Station, the American base at the South Pole. The base is inside a giant dome that keeps everyone warm. I rushed right out to see two of the South Poles. That's right, there's more than one! One is the True Geographic South Pole, which is marked by a simple sign. Another is the Ceremonial South Pole. The Ceremonial South Pole is a short marker surrounded by flags from many countries. The flags are from the United States, the United Kingdom, Norway, and nine other countries. One of the scientists told me that every year they have to move the sign for the True Geographic South Pole. This is because every year the ice we are on slides about 30 feet over the land beneath it. Tomorrow I am leaving the base to visit the Transantarctic Mountains and then the Antarctic Peninsula. I will write from there soon.

November 7

Dear Mom and Dad,

_____

_____

_____

_____

_____

_____

_____

_____

_____

_____

_____

© Harcourt

            Use after reading Chapter 19, Lesson 3, pages 662–667.

Name _____ Date _____

The Pacific Islands and Antarctica

Directions Complete this graphic organizer to show that you understand how to make predictions about the Pacific Islands and Antarctica.

WHAT YOU KNOW	+	WHAT YOU READ	=	PREDICTION	WHAT ACTUALLY HAPPENED

WHAT YOU KNOW +	WHAT YOU READ =	PREDICTION	WHAT ACTUALLY HAPPENED
Europeans changed life for people living in the Americas, Africa, South America, Asia, and Australia.	Pacific Islanders lived in isolation from the rest of the world until early European exploration expanded into the Pacific Ocean.		
The climate in Antarctica is very harsh and cold. This makes it difficult for plants to grow and people to live there. Seals, whales, penguins, and seabirds make Antarctica their home.	Antarctica is surrounded by the waters of the Atlantic, Pacific, and Indian Oceans. These waters support Antarctica's wildlife.		

© Harcourt

19

Name _____ Date _____

Test Preparation

Directions Read each question and choose the best answer. Then fill in the circle for the answer you have chosen. Be sure to fill in the circle completely.

1 The island group that lies north of Australia and east of Indonesia is—
Ⓐ Polynesia.
Ⓑ Hawaii.
Ⓒ New Zealand.
Ⓓ Melanesia.

2 A _____ is a destructive tropical storm that occurs in the South Pacific.
Ⓕ tsunami
Ⓖ typhoon
Ⓗ monsoon
Ⓙ hurricane

3 Which island is a trust territory that is given protection and economic aid by the United States?
Ⓐ New Guinea
Ⓑ Tonga
Ⓒ Solomon
Ⓓ Guam

4 The icy continent of Antarctica has most of the world's supply of—
Ⓕ moss.
Ⓖ uranium.
Ⓗ ice and fresh water.
Ⓙ algae.

5 The emperor or the chinstrap is a species of _____ found in Antarctica.
Ⓐ seal
Ⓑ penguin
Ⓒ whale
Ⓓ albatross

Use after reading Chapter 19, pages 644–669.